PHOBIA

FACING WITH COURAGE

ABOUT THE AUTHOR

Nataly Martinelli is a business administrator and clinical psychologist specializing in the treatment of anxiety disorders. She is committed to sharing her knowledge to help more and more people overcome their fears.

This commitment led her to become one of the pioneers of the clinical use of virtual reality in Brazil, establishing her as a national reference in integrating this technology into psychotherapy—an approach designed to strengthen courage and explored in depth throughout this book.

Passionate about study and continuous professional development, she strives to stay consistently up to date, bringing high-value insights to her courses, lectures, interviews, and articles—and, above all, to this work, which is the result of deep dedication and an unwavering desire to awaken courage in her readers.

ACKNOWLEDGMENTS

First, I thank Life—for teaching me that even pauses carry meaning, and that every detour can reveal a new beginning.

I thank my family for the love that sustains me and reminds me that home is built in the simplest moments, where tenderness becomes strength. Your presence is a daily reminder that love, when shared, expands the soul and gives purpose to every journey.

To everyone who believed in this project: my sincere gratitude for the dedication, excellence, and trust that made it possible. Every act of support—visible or quiet—became part of the energy that allowed this work to be born.

And above all, I thank you, dear reader. May this book be your companion in moments of silence, a lighthouse on cloudy days, and the flame that reminds you of this essential truth: courage is not something you seek outside yourself—it has always lived within you, waiting quietly to be remembered.

INTRODUCTION

There is a moment, in phobia, when the mind is still trying to explain… but the body has already decided. The chest tightens, the breath shortens, the heart accelerates, and reality shrinks. A real threat is not required: a cue, a memory, or a sensation is enough. And then the silent question appears—one many people do not dare to say out loud: "What is happening to me? Why can't I control this?"

This book was written to address that moment: when fear stops being an alarm and begins to take the place of the one who makes decisions. It is for you if fear limits your life and avoidance has become routine; if you want to understand what is happening without blaming yourself; or if you support others and are looking for a clear, humane approach. Here you will find rigor, compassion, and practical resources to move forward step by step.

In these pages, I gathered what I always sought: knowledge drawn from reliable sources, delivered with the dynamism and practicality every reader deserves—whether or not they are a health professional. Because understanding helps, but it is not enough. Phobia is not lack of willpower, nor fragility, nor "drama": it is the body's learning—an automatic response that activates before a person can make a choice. And the way out is not to fight yourself, but to reclaim inner space:

that small place where, even with fear, you can take control of your choices again.

You can read this book as a complete journey—in the proposed order—because each chapter prepares the next: first understanding, then method, then integration. But you can also use individual chapters in the moments that you need them. When fear tightens its grip, go straight to the COURAGE technique and the stabilizing exercises; when you feel steadier, return to the theoretical chapters. There you will understand the avoidance cycle—and how it is broken without violence against yourself. If it helps, keep a notebook nearby. Here, writing is not decoration: it is a way of bringing you back to the present.

Important notice: this book is informational and educational. It does not replace professional evaluation, diagnosis, or treatment. The clinical cases presented have been modified to protect identity and confidentiality.

I did not write this book to explain fear from a distance. I wrote it to bring you a map: to understand it, to hold it, and to reclaim your ability to choose.

My wish is that you, dear reader, may grow into your own strength, one step at a time—a strength you may not yet know you have. It is common to avoid looking at our own shadow, but that momentary discomfort helps us integrate it and move forward.

For that reason, the message I want to leave you with—as you begin this reading, written with such care—is this: allow yourself to know your challenges and, above all, to move through them. Begin to observe your fears from a wide angle—and as you discover their origins, prove to yourself that you are stronger than they are.

To overcome fear is to reclaim the freedom to move beyond it.

FOREWORD

Clinical psychologist Nataly Martinelli, a specialist in the treatment of phobias, fear, and anxiety, writes in a detailed, clear, dynamic, and accessible way. She has the grounded simplicity of someone who truly knows what she is doing—and has done it with excellence for many years. Through brief clinical case accounts, she explains the physical and psychological symptoms most commonly experienced by people living with this condition.

The author adopts a systemic perspective to understand the psychological roots of phobia and introduces a range of therapeutic approaches for its treatment, highlighting, in particular, the innovative use of virtual reality. Those of us who have the privilege of knowing Nataly professionally recognize her creativity, sensitivity, and unwavering dedication to her patients' needs.

In Chapter 4: Facing Challenges Through the COURAGE Technique, the author offers a step-by-step process built around a carefully crafted acronym that helps individuals develop bravery and become more capable of confronting their phobias. The purpose of this book is to help readers understand possible causes of phobia through the workings of the mind—and to persuade them that psychological healing from these distressing symptoms is entirely possible.

I dare to say that this work belongs among the best current contributions to the field. Those who suffer from phobia will find in these pages the assurance that they can reinterpret their misguided and negative emotions. Its usefulness also extends to anyone who lives with or relates to someone with a phobia, offering knowledge and a deeper understanding of this struggle. Psychotherapists, in turn, will find this book to be a valuable source of ideas and techniques to support their patients' treatment.

Teresinha Martins Ferrari
Clinical Psychologist

TABLE OF CONTENTS

1.
AN OVERVIEW OF ANXIETY DISORDERS

In front of me, he breathes with a calm I wish I could feel. The white coat should reassure me, but I can't stop feeling afraid—no matter how safe this place seems. Four completely white, spotless walls. Simple furniture: the chair where I'm sitting and another beside me, a small table between us, his armchair, and to my left, an exam bed. Behind the doctor, a few certificates that should ease the fear rising in me—but they don't. My heart is still racing; it feels as if it might explode out of my chest at any moment. My hands are trembling, and I'm breaking out in a cold sweat unlike anything I've felt before, as my breathing starts to falter.

"Luiza?"

Everything starts to spin. I am sure this fear is going to kill me. And I can't even explain it.

"Luiza? Can you tell me what you're feeling?"

"Sorry, doctor."

I try to explain while I'm trying to breathe, but it feels impossible. Some words won't come; others barely come out, as if speaking and existing at once were simply too hard. My desperate gaze seems to convince him of the seriousness of what's happening, because he immediately orders tests and starts an IV.

Lying on the exam bed, I try to steady myself—even though it doesn't feel like a real option. I close my eyes and keep trying.

Gradually, I begin to breathe normally again. My heart, which had been out of control, now—as they perform the electrocardiogram—begins to settle into a normal rhythm. My hands shake less and, at last, I manage to exhale and thank God I'm still here—after something I still can't name.

As he reviews my symptoms, the doctor explains that I likely experienced a panic attack—or something similar. I had heard a friend mention panic disorder, but she told me anxiety attacks are recurrent in people who receive that diagnosis, so it didn't seem to fit. After all, this was the first time I had ever felt anything so extreme. That was when the doctor explained that panic attacks can appear in different disorders—and not exclusively in panic disorder, as many people believe.

The difference between panic attacks and panic disorder is not only the frequency of episodes, but also the persistent fear of having another one—and the life changes that fear imposes. Hearing that, things began to make more sense.

Still, I wasn't fully convinced that this had anything to do with my emotions. I felt too fine to be going through something like this. It had to be physical.

"Luiza, I recommend you consult a psychologist to evaluate

what's going on, identify triggers, and propose an intervention plan."

The idea scared me a little. I had never been to a psychologist, and I didn't understand why I would need one. But the only thing I was sure of was that I never wanted to live through that again—and I would do whatever it took to avoid it.

I had never felt anything like it. I'll admit it: that morning I was tense when my boss said I would lead the meeting the next day. Imagining a room full of people listening to me made me feel deeply insecure. But that fear was normal, right?

I had spoken in public a few times in my life—especially in college. So speaking didn't seem like the real problem. Over time, I learned that it was enough to take on most of the preparation and let others handle the presentation. That always calmed me down. It wasn't that I couldn't do it. It just wasn't necessary, because I had already done enough for the group. That was what I always told myself.

No matter how hard I tried, I couldn't find the cause of the terrible sensation that sent me to the hospital. Either way, I didn't want to face that terror again. I decided to follow the doctor's recommendation and scheduled a therapy session. The next day, I was there—in the psychologist's office.

"Do you usually feel comfortable in crowded places?"

I'll admit I had to think. Would it be strange to answer that I prefer to be alone? That I avoid events and environments where I feel exposed? That didn't seem unusual to me. It felt more like a personal preference.

"I usually avoid those places… I think I prefer being alone."

At that moment, I remembered my last birthday.

At work, everyone knows I'm shy, and many people understand—especially Marcos. I remember how kind he was to warn me they were planning a surprise party for my birthday. He knows I don't like being the center of attention; he knows what I'm like. I was glad he told me. On the day of the celebration, I took the day off. I hadn't rested in months, so my boss agreed without issue—after all, it was my birthday.

I spent the day alone, like I have in recent years. Of course, I received and replied to several messages, and I felt happy to be remembered. Still, it made me wonder if I had upset Gabriela, my coworker. She didn't call or text; she must have been angry with me for not coming into the office.

That left me unsettled. Even though I wanted to ask her, I felt embarrassed when I saw her the next day. About three days later, she apologized for forgetting my birthday. She explained that her baby hadn't been well and she'd been extremely stressed. Even then, I kept thinking she had been upset with me—and that I should have done something to prevent it.

"Can you recall other episodes where you felt something similar?"

I couldn't remember anything that intense. It's true I had felt palpitations and fear in situations that made me anxious, but nothing like what happened that morning. Little by little, the psychologist helped me bring to mind experiences that seemed ordinary to me—yet were beginning to reveal themselves as part of a single pattern.

Anxiety belongs to all of us. After all, who has not felt anxious before a trip or an exam?

Anxiety is an emotion, like joy or sadness, and—up to a point—it can even be beneficial: it can stimulate creativity and intelligence, becoming fuel for growth and change. It can also be defined as a state of alert in which the body prepares to face unpredictable situations or those perceived as threatening—even when there is no real source of danger.

It is the *recurrence* and *frequency* of anxiety that allow it to be classified as a symptom present in a range of disorders. In anxiety disorders, it appears as a core symptom.

According to data from the World Health Organization (WHO), Brazil is often cited as having one of the highest estimated rates of anxiety disorders, with approximately 18.6 million people affected—about 9.3% of the population.[1]

Now that you understand anxiety is far more common than you might have imagined, let us return to Luiza's case. At any point, did you recognize yourself in what she experienced?

In her interpersonal relationships, Luiza showed an excessive need for approval—something very common in people who struggle with anxiety-related difficulties.

In general, this disproportionate need for approval feeds a sense of imperfection, making the person feel unaccepted by others. But where does that sense of imperfection come from? It is often linked to early experiences in which a child perceives that they must "earn" love or approval; in adulthood, that imprint can shape self-esteem.

That impact on self-esteem is then reinforced by the person themself, who begins to believe that the problems in their life—and in the lives of those around them—are their fault. Luiza, for example, believed her friend had not wished her a happy birthday because she was angry with her, when in fact her friend later apologized and explained: she had forgotten because she was worried about her child. In other words, even with clear evidence, Luiza continued to blame herself and believe she had lost her friend's approval. Her self-esteem was so low that she did not feel accepted by the people around her.

To better understand what Luiza—and perhaps you or someone close to you—may be facing, we will now shift our perspective. First, we will think like Luiza's psychologist. What do her symptoms suggest? What hypotheses come to mind? Next, I will help you organize these hypotheses by clearly explaining the main anxiety disorders.[2]

The main anxiety disorders include:

- Generalized Anxiety Disorder (GAD)
- Obsessive-Compulsive Disorder (OCD)
- Post-Traumatic Stress Disorder (PTSD)
- Panic Disorder
- Agoraphobia
- Specific Phobias
- Social Anxiety Disorder (SAD) or social phobia.

Although this information is technical in nature, I have selected practical, everyday examples that will allow you to step into the mind of someone who lives with these conditions.

1.1 Generalized Anxiety Disorder (GAD)

It may begin as excessive worry—a constant state of irritability, impatience, and apprehension. This is a form of anxiety that persists over time, in which the person feels continuously distressed and worried about multiple issues or activities, rather than being tied to specific situations or objects.

It is worth noting that GAD often emerges in late adolescence and affects women more frequently.[3]

Generalized Anxiety Disorder can originate from worry about a concrete challenge—such as fear of losing a job and being unable to pay the bills at the end of the month. Over time, that anxiety spreads across multiple areas of the person's life, until worry begins to suffocate them—even in situations where there is no proportional reason for concern.

"Are they cheating on me?"

"What if I don't finish the exam on time?"

"What should I serve the friends who are coming over?"

These questions are common and may seem ordinary, but they can conceal an anxious mind. A person with GAD searches for reasons to increase their worry, generating chains of thought. For example, worrying about what to offer guests is normal; however, someone with GAD turns that situation into a major problem.

"I never asked if they're vegetarian! What if they don't like these seasonings? Does Leonardo have any dietary restrictions? Maybe Flavia is pregnant and can't drink. What will they think if the food doesn't turn out well—or burns? Maybe they'll never come again."

Assumptions are the fuel of generalized anxiety.

More than the facts themselves, what keeps anxiety alive in GAD is the relationship the person has with their own thoughts. It is not only thinking too much—it is experiencing those thoughts as real threats that demand an immediate solution. With intolerance to uncertainty, the mind engages in a constant—and exhausting—attempt to control everything.

People with GAD may experience symptoms such as

excessive worry, digestive issues, fatigue, muscle tension, disorientation, and frequent dizziness. In essence, the body is responding to a persistent state of anxiety.

Beyond visible symptoms, it is worth asking what function this anxiety serves in the person's inner life. From a deeper lens, generalized anxiety does not arise only as an "excess of thinking," but as a psychological response to relentless internal demands. Often behind these symptoms lies a need for control—an attempt to protect the individual from a more primitive fear: fear of failing, disappointing, or losing connection with others. When a person does not allow themselves to doubt, make mistakes, or rest psychologically, the body eventually expresses that overload through anxiety.

One of the main challenges GAD can create is the loss of opportunities due to excessive fear of the future. Why does this happen? To avoid the worry associated with being accepted or rejected in a selection process, for instance, the person with GAD may choose not to apply at all. In that way, anxiety closes a door that could have been deeply fulfilling.

1.2 Obsessive-Compulsive Disorder (OCD)

In this anxiety-related disorder, a person experiences repetitive thoughts or behaviors they feel unable to control. Behind this repetition is the sense that something tragic could happen—to themselves or to others—if they fail to carry out certain actions. For example, someone with OCD may develop the compulsive behavior of taking prolonged, repeated showers.

Until the 1980s, OCD was considered a relatively rare

condition. However, studies conducted during that period completely changed that view. Surprisingly, OCD came to rank as the fourth most common disorder, behind only phobias, substance abuse, and depression.[4]

The most common obsessions involve fear of *contamination*, which leads the person to wash repeatedly, *doubt*, which drives repeated checking (such as whether the lights were turned off), and the *need for order* and *symmetry*, which can lead to excessive organizing of objects and spaces.

"I need to wash my hands properly."

"Did I leave the light on?"

"The clothes have to be perfectly organized."

You have probably had one of these thoughts at some point. The difference is that a person with OCD allows these ideas to evolve into actions that, in their mind, can prevent something tragic from happening.

"I'm sure I forgot to turn off the light. I should call someone to check… But what if they don't check properly? I know I left it on. I should go back home."

In addition to returning and confirming the light is off, a person with OCD often repeats the check multiple times, trying to reach the sense of safety they so desperately need. The central problem is that the certainty they seek never arrives. There is always a leftover trace of doubt.

Doubt is OCD's ammunition.

That is why, when we talk about OCD, the most visible symptom is the need to repeat actions. It is not enough to wash your hands once—you may feel compelled to do it ten, twenty, or thirty times. But beyond that, OCD can show up through other common symptoms: racing thoughts, nightmares, persistent obsessions, compulsive and ritualized behaviors, hoarding, and social withdrawal.

In OCD, the mind is not looking for reassurance—it is looking for certainty. And that certainty, paradoxically, never comes.

Beyond what can be observed from the outside, OCD can be understood as an inner experience of extreme responsibility. It is not only fear, but a persistent sense that any lapse, thought, or mistake could have serious consequences for oneself or for others. In this context, repetition is not only about control or perfection—it is an attempt to relieve an anticipated guilt that never truly rests.

Obsessive-Compulsive Disorder can also impact self-esteem and create frustration in interpersonal relationships. This happens because, in many cases, people around the individual do not understand the obsessions, which makes acceptance more difficult. Consider, for example, someone whose compulsion is counting objects. During a conversation, they may very likely divert their attention to count elements in the environment, appearing—though not intentionally—disinterested in the dialogue. Explaining that apparent lack of attention is not always easy.

1.3 Post-Traumatic Stress Disorder (PTSD)

This disorder appears in people who experience intense psychological distress after living through a deeply traumatic event, such as disasters, sexual abuse, or kidnapping. These events act as powerful generators of stress and can trigger a range of anxiety reactions.

Although it is estimated that around 50% of the population will go through some type of traumatic experience over the course of their life, only about 5% to 8% of those individuals will develop PTSD.[5] However, when the trauma is related to childhood abuse, the probability increases significantly: PTSD may affect 36.3% of children who have experienced this form of violence.[6]

A person with PTSD may become extremely hypervigilant, remaining in a constant state of alert out of fear of reliving the trauma.

"This will happen again."
"This time I won't be able to escape."

Many people face traumatic situations—from environmental disasters to armed robberies—and respond in very different ways. Yet in those who develop PTSD, the fear of reliving the traumatic experience takes over completely, even when there is no real evidence that the situation will repeat itself.

"It was raining that day too. The streets were quiet, and it was Wednesday—just like today. That thief will definitely attack me again, but this time he'll use the weapon, not just show it."

The person begins to form associations that are not grounded in concrete facts, but still generate distress and fear. In an effort to protect themselves, they adopt behaviors that offer a momentary sense of safety—such as avoiding walking alone at night, crossing the street upon seeing a man they perceive as physically strong, or avoiding the place where the trauma occurred, even if it requires long detours. But that sense of protection fades quickly.

False associations reinforce trauma.

Beyond the memory of the traumatic event, what becomes fixed in PTSD is the lived experience of extreme helplessness. Trauma is not defined only by what happened, but by the psyche's inability, at that moment, to respond, flee, or protect itself. When the mind cannot symbolize the experience, the past remains open—as if danger were still present. Hyper-vigilance, then, is not an exaggeration, but the psyche's ongoing attempt to prevent it from happening again.

When someone goes through a profoundly traumatic experience and develops this disorder, the mind begins to function in ways that reinforce and reactivate what was lived. For that reason, symptoms such as nightmares, constant agitation, intense stress, intrusive memories, flashbacks, dissociative episodes, panic attacks, loss of interest in daily life, and difficulty regulating emotions are common.

In some cases, PTSD may be associated with hopelessness and thoughts of self-harm or suicide. If this is happening to you, do not stay silent—seek professional help as soon as possible. Despite the intensity of these symptoms, there are therapeutic processes that allow the traumatic experience to be processed and, gradually, a sense of inner safety to be restored.

1.4 Panic Disorder (PD)

Panic disorder is characterized by recurrent panic attacks

with no apparent initial cause. The sensation is so intense that the person begins to fear the onset of a new episode—in other words, they become afraid of fear itself. In some cases, they start avoiding situations that, in their perception, could trigger another crisis. Alongside panic disorder, agoraphobia may also develop.

Panic disorder affects women two to three times more than men and may affect up to 3.5% of the population.[7] It typically emerges in late adolescence and early adulthood, with a low likelihood of appearing in childhood.[8,9]

"My heart is racing."
"I'm going to have an attack."

When we face an unusual situation, it is normal for the heart rate to accelerate—and if that acceleration continues, we may feel as though we are about to have an attack. In PD, however, the episode is not a consequence of being exposed to a fear-inducing situation. The episode begins without explanation—without a trigger that would justify it.

"I don't understand why I feel this way. I was having breakfast and nothing happened. It must be a heart attack— I need a doctor right now. I won't make it in time. This time I'm going to die."

Unexplained panic attacks lead the person to believe that something extremely serious is happening to them. When there is no physical explanation for these reactions, the sense of imminent death intensifies with each new episode.

Death is the imagined certainty that most reinforces fear in panic disorder.

At the root of this fear there is often a profound sense of helplessness. In the middle of a panic attack, the person feels unprotected—as if something terrible were happening inside the body and no resources were available to stop it. This perceived loss of control intensifies terror and makes the experience feel truly life-threatening.

In panic disorder, symptoms are intense and often physical in nature: chest pain, palpitations, rapid and shallow breathing, trembling, sweating, dizziness, nausea, numbness, and abdominal pain. When all of these reactions occur simultaneously, it becomes very difficult to convince someone in the middle of an attack that they are not dying—and that the episode will pass. As this understanding gradually develops, the person can slowly regain the ability to face their fear.

1.5 Agoraphobia

Agoraphobia involves an excessive fear of open spaces, crowds, and situations in which escape might be difficult— such as elevators, shops, concerts, theaters, cinemas, and public transportation, among others. This fear can also arise when the person is alone, even inside their own home.

This disorder is closely related to panic disorder, as mentioned earlier. In fact, approximately two-thirds of people with panic disorder also experience agoraphobia.[10]

"How would I get out if there was a fire?"
"This place is too enclosed."
"There are too many people here."

Recognizing escape routes was once a fundamental

survival skill. Knowing how to leave a dangerous situation was vital information. In agoraphobia, however, the reaction is not limited to fear in the face of imminent danger. Simply being in a place perceived as difficult to leave can be enough to activate anxiety—even when the probability of anything negative happening is minimal or nonexistent.

"Why did they allow another person into this elevator? It's already full—it could fall. How am I going to handle this? All these people in front of me… how will I get out of here? I'd better get off as soon as the doors open."

Even when the destination is still far away, the person with agoraphobia experiences an intense need to "escape" and leave behind the situation that causes discomfort. When escape is not possible, they endure the circumstance with significant suffering and tend to avoid, as much as possible, exposing themselves to that kind of situation again.

Feeling like a hostage—even while free—is part of the daily experience of those living with agoraphobia.

Beyond the apparent fear of certain places, agoraphobia is linked to a gradual erosion of inner safety. What feels threatening is not so much the environment itself, but the anticipation of not being able to find relief if distress arises. In those moments, the body and its reactions stop feeling fully trustworthy. The urge to escape, therefore, is not a rejection of the outside world, but an attempt to protect oneself from an overwhelming internal experience when it does not feel like support is available.

The constant search for escape routes and the active use of them and the avoidance of fear-provoking situations are among the most common manifestations of agoraphobia. In addition, the person often lives in a persistent state of alert and apprehension, accompanied by the physical effects of fear, such as trembling, sweating, and other bodily symptoms.

1.6 Specific Phobias

Specific phobias are characterized by intense, persistent, and out-of-proportion fear in response to a particular object, animal, or situation. When faced with the feared stimulus, the person may react with overwhelming anxiety or rely on avoidance as their primary defense. Avoidance, however, often carries significant costs—including no longer traveling for fear of flying, avoiding friends who have an animal that triggers the phobia, or giving up meaningful everyday experiences.

Research and clinical experience indicate that the most common specific phobias involve animals (such as dogs, spiders, or snakes), natural environments (heights, storms, floods), blood and injections (pain, invasive medical procedures), specific situations (enclosed or open spaces, elevators, airplanes), and other triggers such as vomiting, choking, illness, death, clowns, or certain sounds. Throughout this book, we will explore these recurring phobias in greater depth.

"That dog is going to bite me."
"I don't want to go to the hospital."
"I'd rather take the bus than fly."

Thoughts and phrases like these can also occur in people who do not have a specific phobia. Protecting yourself from potential danger, disliking hospitals, or preferring one mode of transportation are common attitudes. The difference is that, in a phobia, what was once a choice becomes a rigid rule.

"I know it's far away, I'll spend hours on the bus and lose time. The company would pay for the flight and put me in one of the best seats; they were surprised when I refused. They think I'm crazy for turning down this opportunity. But I'll go by bus. Down here I feel safer. The plane would definitely crash if I were on it."

Even when it leads to major losses or meaningful renunciations, a person with a phobia is often willing to give up benefits and opportunities in order to avoid confronting fear. There is a constant conviction that, if they are exposed to the feared situation, the worst will happen. From that belief, the mind builds endless hypotheses to justify why the feared situation must not be faced.

A phobia is often a bond suspended in time: an experience that, when it first emerged, could not be put into words, processed, or integrated with meaning. What remains is a bodily imprint of something still active—something not yet integrated.

In many cases, a phobia protects the person from re-entering an old pain, from confronting anger displaced from its source, or from touching a sadness that, at some point in their story, they learned to silence. The symptom does not arise from weakness, but as an unconscious attempt to preserve psychological balance.

More than an isolated symptom, a phobia can be

understood as an emotional message that became fixed at a particular moment in one's personal history. When that message begins to be heard and processed, the relationship with fear stops being frozen—and can transform.

Phobic symptoms vary considerably depending on the feared stimulus. In general, there is intense avoidance, and when avoidance is not possible, panic-like episodes may arise, triggering physical reactions such as sweating, trembling, palpitations, a sensation of choking, and other manifestations of fear.

In addition to traditional phobias, which we will explore throughout this book, others have emerged that are considered more recent due to their features and their connection with modern life. One of the most debated is nomophobia, understood as the fear of being without electronic devices, and widely discussed in the literature—though it is not a formal diagnosis in the Diagnostic and Statistical Manual of Mental Disorders (DSM-5).

The constant presence of technology in daily life has taken up more and more space and time, fostering, in some cases, dependency patterns that are no longer healthy. Difficulty separating from a mobile phone can gradually become a source of anxiety and distress.

From a deeper perspective, nomophobia is not linked only to the absence of the device, but to the difficulty of holding one's own inner experience without mediation. The phone begins to serve a regulatory function: it soothes anxiety, prevents contact with emptiness, and dampens thoughts or emotions that are hard to tolerate alone. In this way, the fear is not so much about being without the device, but about what emerges when it is no longer available.

If imagining yourself without your phone feels impossible, it may be time to reflect on the place it occupies in your life—and how to restore a more balanced relationship with it.

Fear serves an essential protective function. Problems arise when avoidance becomes the only possible response, shrinking life and limiting choice. Facing fear with awareness, support, and care can open the door to new experiences—and to greater emotional freedom.

1.7 Social Anxiety Disorder (SAD)

Social Anxiety Disorder, also known as social phobia, is characterized by a persistent fear of social exposure—even in small groups or informal situations, such as eating, writing, making eye contact, starting or sustaining a conversation, working, or simply asking a question.

The effects of this disorder can range from avoidance of certain situations to isolation, significantly affecting personal and professional functioning.

"It's better if I stay quiet."
"I'd rather not go if there will be a lot of people."
"I can do it on my own."

It is important to remember that feeling shy or uncomfortable in certain situations does not necessarily mean someone has SAD. In SAD, fear is so intense that it leads the person to avoid social contact out of dread of saying or doing something they consider inappropriate. This pattern is often accompanied by low self-esteem and a constant fear of criticism and rejection, which can progressively limit participation in social settings and gradually erode the development of relational skills.

In SAD, fear is not limited to the interaction itself—it is the fear of being seen. The other person's gaze becomes a constant mirror of judgment, and the individual feels exposed, evaluated, and at risk of being revealed as "not good enough." To protect themselves, attention turns inward; every gesture is monitored, and spontaneity gives way to relentless self-observation.

"Doing this assignment alone is the best option. The only problem is the presentation. Since I don't have a group, I'll have to present by myself. I've got it: I'll prepare the paper and hand it in the next day. I'll lose a few points and say I couldn't come to class."

Creating strategies to avoid social exposure reinforces the phobia, because the person confirms that withdrawing provides momentary relief. Over time, this dynamic fosters progressive isolation.

The more social contact is reduced, the more intense social anxiety tends to become.

Now that we have explored anxiety disorders in greater depth, let us return to Luiza's case. She is still in the office—and you and I are going to help her psychologist narrow the diagnostic possibilities. Generalized Anxiety Disorder? Panic Disorder? Specific phobia? Social Anxiety Disorder?

Based on the symptoms Luiza described, it is already possible to identify which diagnosis best fits her case. Let us consider them in light of her personal history.

Luiza experienced tachycardia, cold sweating, trembling,

facial flushing, headache, nausea, and intense, uncontrollable fear. In isolation, these symptoms could correspond to different anxiety disorders. Yet when we consider her trajectory, we see that the episode was the result of an accumulation of situations she had managed to avoid for years—from not presenting in public during college to, more recently, missing a birthday celebration to avoid being exposed.

This shows that Luiza, without fully realizing it, systematically avoided situations in which she might feel "on display," until those behaviors became integrated into her daily life and explained as a personality trait: shyness. In this context, it is highly likely that she developed SAD.

Social Anxiety Disorder is one of the most common anxiety disorders. Its course is often chronic and requires appropriate treatment for resolution.[11] It generally begins in childhood or adolescence (75% of cases between ages 8 and 15), often after a stressful or humiliating experience. Although it is more prevalent in women, men are the ones who most frequently seek treatment.[12]

Through Luiza's case, it becomes possible to understand how different anxiety disorders can overlap in their manifestations—yet be clearly differentiated when analyzed through the lens of personal history.

Social phobia takes center stage here because it best explains her symptoms and her pattern of avoidance. That said, specific phobias and agoraphobia also affect a significant number of people and can severely limit everyday life, leading to a lifestyle dictated by avoidance.

Phobias are among the most common mental disorders in urban contexts. According to the DSM-5, they are classified into three major groups: specific phobias, social phobia, and agoraphobia.[13] Various studies indicate that between 6.2% and 15.5% of the population has at least one type of phobia. Likewise, the National Institute of Mental Health estimates that between 5.1% and 12.5% of Americans experience one of these conditions.[14]

These data highlight the importance of addressing phobias. Throughout this book, we will explore how knowledge derived from scientific research and clinical practice can guide treatment approaches that reduce the impact of these fears—and help restore a fuller life.

But first, it is essential to understand how fear works. When its protective function is recognized, it becomes possible to distinguish between fear that safeguards and phobia that paralyzes.

2.
UNDERSTANDING FEAR

"The cave you fear to enter holds the treasure you seek."—Joseph Campbell

Fear is more likely to grow where there is no understanding. That is why, in this chapter, I will show you—clearly, visually, and accessibly—what fear is, and how it operates within us.

Put simply and directly: fear is a hardwired neurophysiological state that prepares the body to flee, fight, or freeze. It is a mechanism that has protected us throughout evolution and continues to serve an essential role in our survival. Still, we need to understand the point at which fear helps us live—so that it does not end up doing the opposite and depriving us of a full life.

To understand it better, let us look at fear through its physiology. In the next scene, we will focus on the limbic system, a key network in emotional processing.

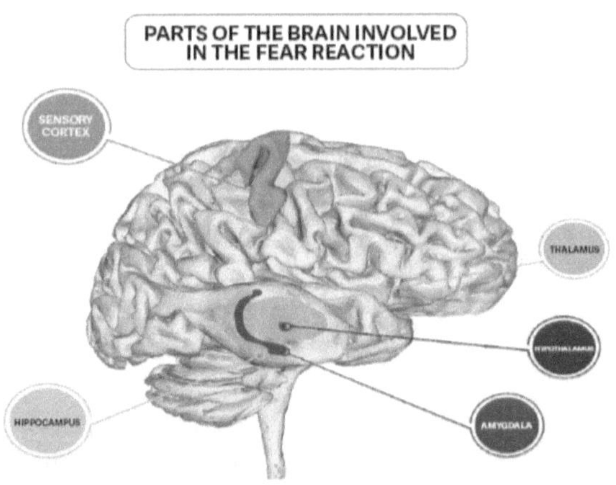

Sensory cortex: interprets sensory information.

Thalamus: relays incoming sensory information (sight, hearing, touch, taste).

Hippocampus: helps place what is happening in context and connect it to conscious memories.

Amygdala: detects threat signals and participates in fear learning, strengthening memories associated with that response.

Hypothalamus: activates the physiological alarm response (fight/flight/freeze).

Now imagine that you are visiting a friend's new home for the first time. Come with me into the scene.

*She opens the gate and you begin to walk in. In front of you, a beautiful garden stretches toward the house. The grass, intensely green, shines under the sunlight. Your friend greets you with a smile and invites you inside. You are happy to be there; it has been a long time since you last saw each other. It feels good to catch up. But suddenly, you hear a bark—**loud, sudden, and sharp.***

In that instant, your startled hearing sends the information to the thalamus. *The* thalamus *relays it to the* amygdala, *which activates rapidly. With the intention of protecting you, the amygdala sounds the alarm: **"We're in danger. Get ready!"** That warning triggers a state of alert.*

In a fraction of a second, the hypothalamus—*already alerted by the* amygdala—*sets the fight-or-flight response in motion. It activates the sympathetic nervous system, which signals the adrenal glands to release adrenaline and norepinephrine. After all, you may need strength in your legs in case you have to run, right? A cascade of chemical and electrical reactions then prepares your body to flee or confront what it perceives as a threat: a potentially dangerous dog that could attack you in the garden.*

Meanwhile, you feel your heart racing, your hands sweating, and an urgent need to escape. The fight/flight/freeze mechanism has been activated successfully. And notice this: all of it happens even before you have seen the dog.

*In the middle of this internal chaos, the hippocampus begins searching for similar memories: **"Have we been through something like this before? Is it truly dangerous?"** At the same time, the prefrontal cortex tries to intervene: **"What's happening? Do we really need to react this way?"***

At that moment, your friend says:

"Don't worry, Fred is on a leash."

Hearing that, you breathe with relief. The hippocampus *recognizes that a leashed dog does not present a risk in this context, and the* prefrontal cortex *finally accepts that there is no real danger. It sends this message to the* hypothalamus:

"We're safe. You can stop now."

You begin to breathe more calmly, and fear slowly recedes. Even when the dog barks again, the mechanism no longer activates in the same way: you are safe, and your brain understands this.

Were you able to grasp how the anatomy of fear works? Of course, this entire process happens in a fraction of a second. In fact, you took longer to read this story than you would to experience it. I have simplified the fear pathway to make it easier to follow—because understanding it makes it much easier to manage.

But now imagine that neither the *hippocampus* nor the *prefrontal cortex* manages to stop the *hypothalamus*. Fear remains active, the sense of danger intensifies, and the body's urge to flee, fight, or freeze persists. It is within this dysregulated fear that phobia can take root.

Fear is a protective response; phobia disrupts it and leaves the person feeling exposed and vulnerable.

A person with a specific animal phobia, for example, cannot interrupt the fear response even if someone tells them the dog is on a leash. The barking freezes them; they imagine the animal breaking free, recall previous traumatic experiences, or anticipate dangers that reinforce the fear. In this moment, the exact cause of the phobia matters less than the fact that the body reacts as if there were real danger, despite there being none, obeying the brain's alarm signal.

If we widen this reflection, we see that fear arises in the presence of a threat—real or interpreted. When that threat is understood as harmless, the reaction stops. So far, it seems clear.

But not all fears are tied to a real physical presence. In the earlier example, a dog provoked fear. Yet have you noticed how many fears appear in response to objects, situations, or people that, in reality, pose no danger?

Fear of a lion protects your life. But does fear of public speaking do the same? You do not need to flee or fight the people listening to you—and yet the knot in your stomach and the dread still shows up. Why?

Because we no longer live in the jungle or in a natural environment filled with constant, real threats. You know that, but your brain does not. So in everyday situations, it interprets that your life is at risk and activates the same mechanism described in the story with the barking dog.

From this perspective, imagine if you felt no fear at all. How would you cross a street? What precautions would you take near a cliff? Where would you find the strength to run from an attacker?

Feeling fear is completely normal. The difference between fear and phobia is often found in intensity, frequency, and—above all—impact: how much it interferes with life and how much avoidance it demands.

There is also a fine line between fear and excitement. Fear can make us feel alive, and perhaps that is why some people seek adrenaline. Even if it seems contradictory to associate fear with something positive—just think of horror films, amusement parks, or extreme sports.

Enjoying fear in moderate doses can be part of a healthy experience. In those contexts, fear is contained within control and safety: the person knows they can stop, leave, or step off. That is why a feeling of intensity, accomplishment, or emotional release can emerge.

But when fear stops being occasional and begins to occupy a central place in inner life, it loses its protective function and starts to restrict. In those cases, learning to manage it becomes essential.

Managing fear does not mean eliminating it. It means accepting it—and developing resources that allow the *hippocampus* and the *prefrontal cortex* to interrupt the reaction when the situation is not truly dangerous.

So how does that happen in practice?

When you heard the bark the second time, you no longer felt fear. Why? For at least for two reasons.

1.   You remembered (and understood) that a leashed dog could not harm you in that context.
2.   You had already lived through a similar moment, and your body confirmed that nothing bad happened.

This affirms something you have probably heard before: we need to face our fears in order to master them—rather than be mastered by them.

A line often attributed to Aristotle captures this well: "I consider the one who conquers his fears braver than the one who conquers his enemies, for the hardest victory is over oneself."

Overcoming fears is not simple. But each time you choose

to face them instead of running, you reclaim the steering wheel of your own life.

2.1 The Cognitive Triad

Cognitive-behavioral therapy (CBT) emphasizes the present. The therapist helps the person face current challenges by observing how thoughts influence emotions and behavior. Many times, distress begins there—in the interpretation of what we live.

From that foundation comes a core concept in **cognitive therapy**: the cognitive triad. This model describes the dynamic relationship between thoughts, emotions, and behavior. What **we think** influences what **we feel**, and what we feel shapes how **we act**.

You may wonder why I am bringing this triad into a chapter about fear. This will become clear if we think about Marília, who has an intense fear of flying. Marília has not been on an airplane in many years—not because she went through a traumatic experience, but because she anticipates a catastrophe that, to her, feels unquestionable: the plane will crash into the sea. This conviction is not supported by objective data, but by an internal interpretation her mind has built and keeps active.

Even before she reaches the airport, her body responds. Her heart rate accelerates, her breathing becomes shallow, and tension rises in a way that is hard to control. The danger does not exist yet—but the fear response has already been triggered.

If we observe the cognitive triad in this case, the process becomes clear.

1. Marília thinks the plane will crash into the sea.

2. That thought activates an intense emotional and physiological fear response.

3. As a consequence, she develops avoidance behavior, choosing long bus trips instead of facing a flight.

This example shows how fear does not arise only from external circumstances, but from the mind's interpretation of them. From that interpretation, behaviors are created that reinforce a phobia and maintain it over time.

Understanding this mechanism is fundamental to understanding fear. Thoughts can trigger intense reactions even in hypothetical situations in which no real danger exists.

Being inside an elevator, for example, is not objectively a threat. And yet the mind can generate a series of thoughts capable of activating fear.

"What if the door doesn't open when I reach my floor?"
"This elevator is old—it could fall."
"If the power goes out, I'll be trapped."

None of these scenarios has happened or is likely to happen. And still, the body reacts as if the danger were real. The fight/flight/freeze mechanism activates, and even if those hypotheses never materialize—because they are distorted thoughts—the person remains trapped in a state of fear.

At this point, identifying and learning to manage automatic thoughts becomes essential. These thoughts appear quickly in response to situations that create discomfort and, if they are not questioned, they can determine what we do next.

That is why they need to be brought into the rational plane.

When fear arises, it helps to pause and observe the thoughts that come with it. From there, questions such as these can be useful.

- Is what I am thinking based on facts?
- Statistically speaking, how likely is this to happen?
- Is there a real and immediate threat to my life?
- Have I experienced similar situations without harm?

When automatic thoughts are questioned, their influence over emotion weakens. The person begins to recognize that it is not the situation itself that generates fear, but a distorted interpretation of reality.

However, when we are talking about phobia, this process requires deeper attention. Phobia is marked by a sense of losing control: the person cannot explain the intensity of the fear, and precisely because they do not understand it, they cannot regulate it alone. Unlike everyday fear, which serves an adaptive function, phobia often requires treatment.

When should you seek help? When the mere idea of facing the feared object or situation causes intense anxiety; when avoidance becomes the main strategy for regulating distress; and when, if avoidance is not possible, the experience results in suffering, anguish, and a persistent sense of threat.

In searching for help, many people hope to eliminate fear completely. But overcoming a phobia does not mean eradicating fear—it means learning to relate to it in a conscious and rational way.

Overcoming a phobia is possible, and it is closely tied to self-knowledge. It involves understanding not only your current relationship with fear, but also your emotional history, learned patterns, and the relational contexts in which that fear was built.

When a person learns to see themselves more broadly and understand the deeper reasons behind the behaviors they maintain, facing fear stops feeling like an impossible threat—and becomes a path of transformation.

Knowing yourself—your fears, experiences, and history—requires impartial observation and an honest analysis of your relationship with the world. That is why, in addressing phobia, it is essential to consider not only the individual, but also the family and relational systems that are part of their story.

To close this chapter, choose a situation you usually avoid out of fear. Write down the following.

1. What you fear will happen.
2. What your body does when you imagine it.
3. What you do to relieve it (your avoidance).

For now, simply observe with honesty. What is seen clearly has already begun to change shape. And when fear stops being an enigma, an unavoidable question emerges: how did you learn to carry it—and in which relationships was it reinforced?

3.
PERSONAL PROFILE AND FAMILY SYSTEMS

Have you noticed that not all phobias are the same? Some show up in social settings, others in open or enclosed spaces, and many cluster around very specific objects or situations. Given this diversity, I chose to focus this book on specific phobias—not only because of their high prevalence (affecting roughly 11% of the general population[1]), but because of the silent, profound way they can restrict a person's life.

A specific phobia is not defined only by fear, but by the way fear begins to organize life. The person learns to avoid situations they perceive as dangerous even when the real risk is minimal or nonexistent. Over time, what started as a protective response, stops being a choice and becomes a rigid rule that limits freedom.

In this pattern, fear rarely appears in isolation. It is often accompanied by intense anticipatory anxiety that activates even before the situation occurs. The body reacts as if danger were already present: trembling, shortness of breath, sweating, palpitations, gastrointestinal discomfort, or a sudden sense of losing control may arise—sometimes escalating into panic-like episodes. Psychologically, catastrophic thoughts, difficulty concentrating, intense emotional distress, fear, anger, or shame are common.

Beyond these manifestations, there is a less visible—but clinically essential—aspect. People with specific phobias often share a similar psychological profile, and that profile is rarely built in isolation. In many cases, it is deeply intertwined with family systems and early relational experiences, shaping how fear is learned, maintained, and transmitted. Throughout this chapter, we will begin to unravel how that link is established.

Because of the wide variety of specific phobias, this book deliberately focuses on those that appear most frequently: **animal phobia, blood/needle phobia, fear of flying**, and **claustrophobia**, as well as their most common associations with **agoraphobia**. In each case, the goal will not be merely to describe fear, but to understand the psychological and relational profile that sustains it over time.

3.1 Animal Phobia

Intense and persistent fear in the presence of animals or insects (dogs, spiders, snakes, cockroaches, among others).

From a very early age, we learn which animals are considered dangerous, threatening, or repulsive. These messages are rarely neutral. They are transmitted through tone of voice, facial expressions, sudden warnings, and family stories that associate certain animals with danger. Over time, fear is not only learned—it becomes embodied. This helps explain why animal phobias are so prevalent. A large study in the United States with more than 8,000 participants found that 22.2% of people reported fear of animals—a higher proportion than fear of heights, storms, enclosed spaces, or blood.[2]

Animal phobia often begins in childhood and affects women about twice as often as men.[3] Within that difference lies a particular way of living with fear: as early warning, as constant attention to the environment, as an attempt to anticipate the unpredictable. Fear does not remain an idea; it settles into the body and begins to organize daily experience.

Once fear is internally organized, certain stimuli gain special power. Features such as size, sudden movement, speed, unpredictability, sound, or physical appearance can intensify the fear response. Yet what maintains the phobia over time is rarely the animal itself—it is the way the person learns to relate to what cannot be controlled.

In an effort to feel safe, many people reorganize their behavior. They cross the street, constantly scan the environment, avoid certain places, flee at the slightest hint of contact, or establish rigid routines to reduce unpredictability. In some cases, avoidance becomes symbolic: the feared animal cannot even be named. These strategies bring immediate relief, but they also reinforce fear. Distance offers the illusion of control— while fear grows silently. Paradoxically, the greater the distance from what is feared, the more intense the fear becomes.

To understand how this dynamic develops in real life, we must look beyond the animal and attend to the meaning it takes on in the person's inner world.

In many cases, animal phobia is linked to an early experience in which something broke in suddenly—without warning, without the possibility of anticipation or control. It may have been an unexpected threat, or a situation experienced as invasive, overwhelming the person's capacity to understand or respond at the time. Fear did not disappear. It was registered and remained in the body as an alarm signal—reactivated whenever something unpredictable, invasive, or uncontrollable appeared again.

From this place, certain animals take on a particular symbolic weight. They often represent what cannot be negotiated or reasoned with: instinct, aggression, unpredictability, and the invasion of personal boundaries. The phobia points to the place where the psyche attempts to protect itself from repeating an experience that, at its origin, exceeded available resources. The body remembers what the mind could not yet symbolize.

When this fear structure sets in, it is not always conscious. Often it shows up in everyday choices, silences, and renunciations that seem small, but end up organizing a life.

Case 1: Maria

Maria's story makes it possible to see how this process becomes embodied in one person's experience.

Maria is 37 years old. When she sees a dog, fear appears immediately. She has crossed the street countless times just imagining that it might bark—or worse, attack her. The animal does not need to come close: the scene activates much earlier, in her body.

She remembers clearly when this fear began. She was six years old when a neighbor's dog barked suddenly right next to her ear. It was brief, but overwhelming. From that moment on, fear settled in like a constant presence. Yet not all her memories with animals are negative. She still holds affectionate memories of her grandmother's dogs, with whom she lived for a time.

Maria currently lives with her mother and siblings, but she does not want to stay there. Dependence feels suffocating to her. She needs everything to be under control and hates unexpected changes. Recently, her sister's unplanned visit disrupted the family routine and stirred intense irritation.

And yet, when asked what she felt, she chose to stay silent. For her, expressing emotion equals exposure. Showing what she feels is experienced as being seen in her vulnerability.

3.2 Blood and Needle Phobia

Fear related to medical procedures such as injections, blood tests, wounds, or direct exposure to an injured body.

A certain discomfort with blood, needles, or physical pain is part of being human. But when this discomfort intensifies and becomes persistent, it begins to interfere significantly with daily life—affecting health care and generating psychological suffering.

This phobia has a distinctive feature that sets it apart from others: the possibility of fainting in response to the feared stimulus. It often comes with nausea, dizziness, or a sudden wave of weakness that can culminate in syncope.

Physiologically, the reaction often begins with an intense

activation—raised heart rate, sweating, tension—and then, after a few moments, drops sharply. Heart rate and blood pressure decrease abruptly, reducing oxygenation to the brain and producing pallor, blurred vision, vertigo, or fainting. This sudden bodily response is experienced not only as confusing, but as a sudden loss of control over one's own body.

In this phobia, the body is not responding only to the blood or the needle, but to the entire scene that activates: the body exposed, observed, and physically "entered" by someone else in a context of care. What is meant to protect is experienced as invasive, and what promises safety awakens threat. Fainting is not an organism "failure," but an extreme form of interruption: when the experience becomes psychologically impossible to sustain, the body withdraws and sets a limit where words cannot.

Another relevant aspect is its strong family component. In many cases, fear does not appear in isolation—it is transmitted across generations, not only through biology, but through gestures, silences, and narratives that shape how the family relates to the body, pain, and illness.

In one study, 61% of people with blood phobia and 29% of those with needle phobia reported first-degree relatives with similar fears, suggesting a heritable vulnerability combined with relational learning and family modeling.[4]

Case 2: Clara

Clara's story helps us to understand how this fear organization expresses itself not only in the body, but in the way a person lives, cares for herself, and occupies a role within the family.

Clara is 27 years old. The very idea of going to a hospital triggers intense fear, so she avoids it whenever she can. She cannot remember the last time she went. She has not had a blood test in four years, and she has not received a vaccine in six.

Clara does not experience this as something purely personal. Her mother and grandmother share the same fear. She even wonders whether it is "a family thing." For much of her childhood, she lived with her grandmother, who cared for her in a constant, protective way.

In daily life, Clara demands perfection of herself. She strives to meet every expectation and maintain control, even though inwardly she feels fragile and insecure. Even after placing third in the admissions ranking for a public university, the feeling of inadequacy persisted.

Within her family, Clara holds a position of reverence. She feels she must sustain it. Maintaining control has become a form of protection: do not fail, do not fall, do not be exposed. Yet the very control that gives her safety ends up limiting her health and well-being.

3.3 Fear of Flying (Aerophobia)

Fear of flying can present as an intense and persistent specific phobia in response to air travel.

Although for many people flying represents mobility and expansion, for others it becomes profoundly destabilizing—capable of generating suffering, avoidance, and a constant sense of losing control. Studies suggest that between 10% and 40% of people in industrialized countries experience some degree of tension when flying, showing that this discomfort—while not always a phobia—is more common than is typically acknowledged.[5]

Along these lines, Ekeberg and colleagues (1990) identified three frequent profiles in fear of flying:

- those who have never flown;
- those who fly as little as possible and experience distress before and during the flight;
- and those who feel ongoing apprehension—mild, moderate, or intense: they do not avoid travel, but the experience becomes unpleasant.

This fear may manifest as a primary phobia, when the airplane becomes the central object of fear, or emerge as a secondary expression of other fears that overlap and amplify one another. In many cases, what activates is not only the possibility of an accident, but fear of enclosed spaces, heights, instability, becoming ill mid-flight, losing control of the body, being trapped among strangers, or flying over vast stretches of water without clear reference points.[6]

But reducing aerophobia to these visible elements is often insufficient. Behind the declared fear of the airplane, a deeper experience frequently unfolds. Flying involves leaving solid ground, relinquishing control for a time, and accepting a suspended state: there is no immediate return, no ground under your feet, and no way to intervene actively if something happens. For some people, this reactivates an older fear: the fear of being without support.

In those cases, fear of flying may be linked less to the sky than to separation—separation from home, familiar bonds, and the spaces that organize emotional identity. The airplane does not only cross the air; it crosses a symbolic threshold. It forces a departure from the protective field in which safety was once guaranteed by proximity, repetition, and control.

From this perspective, fear is directed not so much at real risk as at the inner experience flight imposes: a temporary suspension of support, an autonomy that feels forced—and for which the person does not always feel prepared. That is where the flight scenario gains its destabilizing power.

Often it is not the airplane itself that destabilizes, but what flying puts at stake: the impossibility of control, the distance from known anchors, and the confrontation with an identity that, for a few hours, loses its immediate ground.

Case 3: Talita

Talita's story helps us understand how this process takes shape in a person's lived experience.

Talita is 34 years old. She remembers clearly when the difficulty began. She was fourteen and returning from the United States when, during a domestic flight, she suddenly felt very unwell. The episode was intense and overwhelming. From then on, flying stopped being neutral and became associated with discomfort, anticipation, and fear.

Over time, travel became increasingly difficult. Talita realized she needed help when, during a conference, she could not gather enough courage to fly back home. On another occasion, trying to confront the fear without preparation, she decided to fly. The experience felt extreme: intense nausea, a sense of losing bodily control, and constant worry about disturbing the people around her—even while unable to regulate what she felt.

Later, after her divorce, Talita recognized a pattern running through different areas of her life. In the relationship, as in flight, there was a constant need for control and a silent pressure not to fail. Tolerating instability, uncertainty, and the possibility of losing control felt deeply threatening.

3.4 Claustrophobia and Agoraphobia

Claustrophobia is related to the fear of enclosed spaces, such as elevators, airplanes, cars, or rooms without a clearly visible exit.

Claustrophobia is not only the physical space, but the inner experience of being trapped—with no immediate possibility of escape. In many cases, this fear is accompanied by a sensation of not getting enough air—one of the most common concerns in this type of phobia.[7] Elevators and airplanes often become the most feared settings, not because of the place itself, but because of the absence of an immediate exit and the feeling of closure they evoke.[8]

It is estimated that about 10% of the population feels uncomfortable in enclosed spaces, and around 2% experience the phobia in a severe form. In more intense cases, roughly 33% report onset in childhood.[9]

Claustrophobia may also appear alongside agoraphobia, understood as a persistent fear of being in places with many people, such as concerts, public transportation, cinemas, or lines, where leaving would not be easy. In these cases, the fear is not only about "being there," but about becoming ill, fainting, or not receiving help in the event of sudden incapacitation.[10]

Beyond the place itself, what activates is an inner experience of helplessness. Claustrophobia is not only about walls; it is about a tightening from within, as if the body had no margin and the mind had no air. Agoraphobia, in turn, intensifies exposure: the possibility that fragility will happen in front of others, without private shelter. In both cases, fear organizes itself around the same core: the experience of being overwhelmed without support.

In many cases, claustrophobia is not limited to enclosed spaces, but resonates with early relational experiences. Highly controlling families, environments where separation was experienced as dangerous, or bonds in which there was no space for disagreement can leave a deep imprint. The fear of being trapped reappears not only in front of closed doors, but in situations that reactivate the feeling of having no psychological exit.

It is not uncommon for these phobias to organize around the fear of having a panic attack without access to help. In such cases, the presence of a trusted figure often becomes central, serving as an anchor against the experience of inner disintegration.

When this kind of fear takes hold, it begins to reorganize daily life. Routes are avoided, places are ruled out, and decisions are made not based on desire, but on the constant attempt to prevent panic.

Case 4: Jéssica

Jéssica's story helps us understand how this dynamic beb comes embodied in one person's experience.

Jessia is 26 years old. Since the age of ten, she has lived with intense anxiety in response to enclosed spaces, elevators, airplanes, and even crowds. The reaction appears abruptly and takes over her body before she can organize a rational response.

She remembers periods in which she went days without leaving home. The mere idea of being around people felt unbearable. That experience brought back childhood memories, when speaking in front of the class produced paralyzing anguish.

One of her most striking memories is an image of a fire near her home in which someone died. That episode left a persistent imprint, associated with fear of not being able to escape in time.

During childhood, her relationships with her siblings were conflictual. Yet whenever disputes arose, her mother would intervene to protect her. That protective figure offered calm and relief. In adulthood, that protection is no longer available in the same way, and Jéssica feels vulnerable and insecure.

Although she performs well academically, she rarely feels "enough." She engages in constant self-monitoring and experiences a persistent fear of losing control. For that reason, she avoids alcohol and avoids situations that might weaken her inner sense of command.

From this perspective, claustrophobia and agoraphobia do not appear as isolated fears of spaces or crowds, but as structured responses to the experience of being without support. Fear settles in when external protection is no longer guaranteed and the person faces the demand of self-regulation without external anchors.

3.5 Fear of Heights, Fear of Flying, and Aerophobia: A Connection with Balance

These are different phobias, yet they share a common underlying axis: **balance**. How does that relationship form?

Several studies indicate that the development of fear of heights, aerophobia, and agoraphobia may be related to alterations in postural control and balance. This means that some people rely more heavily on visual and bodily supports to remain stable, due to less efficient integration of vestibular, visual, and proprioceptive signals.[11]

The vestibular system—a set of structures in the inner ear responsible for spatial orientation and the perception of movement—must coordinate with those supports to maintain bodily stability. When that integration is compromised, the sense of inner security may weaken.

In certain environments—such as elevated, open, or suspended spaces—visual and bodily reference points diminish significantly. For those who depend more on these anchors, the experience can feel like sudden exposure to vulnerability: the body is perceived as unanchored, unsupported, with an immediate sense of risk of falling. It is not only the physical environment, but the internal experience of losing stability that must be considered.

This bodily sensation of insecurity can activate the fear response. When repeated over time, it can contribute to the development of phobias such as fear of heights, fear of flying, or fear of open spaces—showing that in some cases the symptom is also sustained by a physiological component, even when no clearly identifiable traumatic event exists.

3.6 A Recurring Profile Beneath Different Phobias

As we observe the clinical profiles presented throughout the book, traits begin to emerge that repeat beyond the phobic object. Among them, the following are frequently highlighted:

- an intense need for control
- a persistent sense of insecurity
- low self-esteem
- difficulty expressing emotions
- high levels of self-demand
- perfectionistic traits
- contained anger
- difficulty allowing vulnerability
- previous experiences of overprotection.

These traits do not operate in isolation or by chance. When they appear persistently, they often point to a particular emotional organization that goes beyond the feared object and begins to explain how the person relates to themselves and to others. It is within this internal organization that phobia takes on its function.

Reading these characteristics, it becomes difficult not to recognize them in the stories presented so far. The need for control, for example, shows up in Maria, who becomes distressed by visits for fear of losing command of the situation, or in Jéssica, who avoids alcohol out of fear of losing control over her actions. Ordinary situations in daily life can become powerful sources of anxiety for those living with phobia.

Persistent insecurity and low self-esteem are often deeply connected. Those who do not trust their own inner resources rarely feel prepared to face the unpredictable, which intensifies the experience of threat. This insecurity also shows up in difficulty communicating feelings. In Maria's case, expressing emotion feels like exposure; out of fear of appearing fragile, she chooses silence.

It is also common for these individuals to maintain high levels of self-demand. Even when objective results confirm competence—exam approvals, academic performance, professional achievements—an inner sense of inadequacy persists. The constant effort toward perfection lives side by side with an ongoing fear of failing, as seen in Clara, who felt her work was "never good enough."

From a neurobiological perspective, psychiatrist Daniel Amen has described that in some patients with phobias and/or panic disorder, increased activation may be observed in the basal ganglia—deep brain structures involved in anticipation, action initiation, and alarm circuitry.[12] Along similar lines, profiles marked by high self-demand (for example, in high-performance environments) have also been associated with greater activation in this region, which may resonate with several traits observed in phobic profiles.

Another frequent element is difficulty expressing anger. Conflict is avoided, emotions are contained, and tension accumulates. From a psychodynamic reading, this pattern reflects unprocessed emotional conflicts—especially when affects such as anger, sadness, or frustration were difficult to recognize or express within significant bonds. What could not be spoken then finds an indirect route of expression, displaced onto an external object that becomes the container for fear.[13]

By avoiding conflict and "storing" anger, the person accumulates tension that, over time, demands release—often in more intense ways.

This contained emotional load can affect relationships—with family, friends, and the environment, but it especially impacts the person themself, who must live with elevated levels of stress, anxiety, irritability, and fear, creating fertile ground for phobic symptoms to persist.

For this reason, they often avoid showing themselves and expressing what they feel, because emotional expression is linked—in their lived experience—to exposure and risk. Needing control and appearing strong becomes a form of protection against the fear of inner collapse. Often, this defense conceals a deeper lack: having been overprotected at some point in life can foster a dependency the person does not want to acknowledge—to others or to themself.

From this perspective, the importance of studying profiles becomes clear. This analysis allows us to identify common patterns among people with phobias.

When these patterns are recognized, treatment can become more precise and effective, because although phobic objects vary greatly, the emotional profiles that sustain them are often remarkably similar. In this way, understanding origins becomes more accessible.

While there is no single scientific proof that conclusively explains the origin of phobias, literature and clinical experience converge on the interaction of multiple factors. Traditionally, traumatic, genetic, and environmental factors are highlighted.[14] Other relevant elements also come into play, such as intrauterine and physiological factors, identified through clinical observation and professional practice, which expand our understanding of the phobic phenomenon.

- **Traumatic factor**: when the person goes through a significant negative experience, lived as overwhelming or threatening.
- **Genetic factor**: transmission of predispositions that can increase vulnerability to fear.
- **Intrauterine factor**: maternal influence during gestation, especially in contexts of intense stress.
- **Physiological factor**: bodily or sensory alterations that influence fear perception and the organism's response
- **Environmental factor**: fear learning through observation, coexistence, or significant relational models

When we consider the **traumatic factor**, the mechanism becomes more evident. For example, someone who experiences intense turbulence during a flight may develop fear of flying and fear of facing that experience again. In that case, aerophobia emerges as a consequence of a traumatic event. However, it is important to emphasize that not every traumatic factor is directly related to the feared object; sometimes, fear functions as a displaced expression of a prior emotional experience that was not psychologically processed.

Beyond the impact of traumatic experiences, clinical and genetic research has shown that specific phobias have a significant familial component. First-degree relatives of a person with a phobia have a higher risk of developing this type of symptom compared to relatives of people without a history of psychopathology (31% versus 11%).[15]

In addition to traumatic and genetic factors, there is a third element less explored: the **intrauterine factor**.

This factor relates to intrauterine programming—a crucial time in the constitution of human life. In this context, everything the mother feels, thinks, imagines, or experiences is also lived by the baby she is carrying. The baby, fragile and dependent, inhabits its first home: the maternal body.

Maternal anxiety, for example, is expressed through hormones and neurotransmitters that circulate in the bloodstream, reach the placenta, and ultimately the fetus.[16] In this way, family begins to influence the individual even before the individual can be conscious of themselves. In this sense, Lewin (1935) related claustrophobia to anxieties experienced by the baby in the uterus, who tends to defend itself by curling into a fetal position—a reaction frequently seen during anxiety crises.[17] This observation highlights the connection between gestational experience and the development of fear.

Recall our earlier discussion of vestibular influence in fear of flying, heights, and agoraphobia. Alterations in the balance system can make a person more vulnerable to developing these phobias. This reinforces the idea that bodily constitution can also influence the emergence of anxiety disorders.

Yet influence does not stop there. From the **environmental factor**, we understand that the setting in which a person develops can either favor—or not—the emergence of a phobia, as well as other psychological disorders.

When genetic, intrauterine, and environmental factors are considered together, family systems take on a central role. Why?

The intrauterine factor is a direct, undeniable bond between mother and child. Genetics, in turn, tangibly connects members of the same family. And the family environment is, without question, the context with the greatest influence on emotional formation. There is no environment that marks us more deeply than our own family.

Our first contact with the world happens through family figures. Parents, siblings, grandparents, or caregivers often transmit—without realizing—beliefs, fears, and ways of relating that can facilitate the development of a phobia. Clara shared that her mother and grandmother carried the same fear of blood. How many times might she have witnessed vaccines avoided or medical care postponed? Indirectly, fear moved from generation to generation until it reached her own experience.

For this reason, treatment for specific phobias involves the patient understanding the role family plays in their recovery process. What does that mean?

In some cases, treatment may include a family member being physically present in a session. But the goal goes beyond that. The patient needs to recognize how family bonds influence the way they live and sustain the phobia.

Consider Jéssica. She reports fear of enclosed spaces, such as airplanes—a fear also present in her mother. When she speaks about it with her mother (who is not in treatment), her insecurity may be reinforced, because her mother tends to justify her own fear by bringing up accidents or turbulence episodes. In that way, Jéssica's phobia is consolidated.

The opposite situation is also not uncommon. If Jéssica tells her brother she went fifteen days without leaving home, she may be criticized or misunderstood. Again, the phobia is reinforced—feeding anguish and deepening isolation.

It is not accidental, then, that Jéssica feels capable of facing the feared object only when accompanied by trusted people—family or friends, which is directly linked to agoraphobic symptoms.

Therapeutic work with the family system does not focus only on other people's reactions, but on the way the patient responds to those reactions. In this sense, it is not only the environment's behavior that determines outcomes, but how the person interprets it, internalizes it, and inscribes it into their emotional history.

When this process becomes conscious, facing one's fears stops feeling impossible and becomes a complex—but workable—challenge. Phobia does not originate in the external stimulus itself, but in the way the mind anticipates it, interprets it, and fixes it as a threat.

In this sense, phobia can be understood as an internally constructed intensification of fear, sustained by beliefs, learning, and emotional memory. That is why transformation does not depend on external changes, but on the person's ability to review, reinterpret, and reorganize the meaning fear has acquired throughout their relational and psychological history.

The same logic applies to emotional development in childhood.

3.7 Raising Children Without Phobias

No parent or caregiver wants a child to develop a phobia—whether in childhood or later in adulthood. And yet, as we have seen, family systems can unintentionally facilitate the emergence of fear. Recognizing this reality is what led me to write this section: to offer adults conscious, practical resources to emotionally protect their children.

Some parents end up repeating patterns. Many of these patterns are not transmitted consciously—they are emotionally inherited across generations, as automatic responses to fears that were never processed. In childhood, these experiences are not recorded only as memories, but as emotions and ways of responding that become part of a person's emotional story.

Sometimes, fear is instilled as a form of control or reprimand through phrases repeated in everyday life, such as: "If you move away from me, someone will come and take you," or "If you throw a tantrum, I'll leave you here alone."

Simple phrases—but capable of leaving a lasting emotional imprint, because they land at a stage of development when the child does not yet have the resources to distinguish exaggeration from real threat.[18]

In these cases, fear does not originate in the literal content of the words, but in the emotional experience surrounding them: the absence of safety, emotional holding, and the feeling of being welcomed and protected in early bonds.[19] Many of the intense fears we develop are anchored in this early stage, often inaccessible to conscious memory. And it is precisely here that the role of parents becomes decisive.

When an adult's fear is not recognized or processed, it tends to be transmitted to the child without mediation— through everyday language, attitudes, and the emotional climate that shapes the relationship. Under these conditions, fear stops serving an adaptive function and begins to organize the child's experience around restriction and avoidance.

Raising emotionally secure children does not mean protecting them from all discomfort, but offering a presence capable of holding it. Fear is part of being human; the adult's task is to help it be recognized, symbolized, and transformed within the bond.

From this place, emotional security is not built by eliminating fear, but through a relationship that listens, understands, and accompanies without invalidating the child's experience. To support this understanding, below are some of the most common fears by developmental stage.[20,21]

3.7.1 Common Fears by Developmental Stage

0 to 6 months
- Loud or unexpected noises
- Loss of physical support or holding

6 to 18 months
- Unfamiliar people and situations
- Separation from attachment figures
- Heights

2 to 3 years
- Animals
- Large or imposing objects

3 to 6 years
- Darkness
- Masked people
- Storms
- Prolonged separation or fear of losing parents

6 to 10 years
- Imaginary beings (monsters, ghosts)

- Social exposure (speaking in class, participating in public)
- Bodily injury
- Supernatural phenomena

10 to 12 years
- Physical appearance
- Death or loss of a loved one
- Friendship bonds

Age 13 and up
- Autonomy, independence, and life projects
- Fear of making mistakes
- Rejection
- Interpersonal relationships

Accepting the existence of fear is part of emotional development. What can be held in childhood does not disappear—it transforms.

Often, accompanying a child means finding ways to approach what scares them without naming it too directly. The child's world better understands ideas that arrive through images, gestures, and simple stories—where fear can appear without invading and courage can emerge without being forced.

A story can say what does not need to be explained.

3.7.2 Bella's Story

In a forest, many small animals lived happily, each with their own tasks. Among them was Bella, a brightly colored butterfly who loved to fly from one flower to another.

One day Bella looked down and saw a green toad moving through the flowers. He was strong and loud, and he scared her.

Bella's fear was so big that she stopped flying. She stopped visiting her beautiful garden and began to stay close to home. She did not want the toad to spot her.

Then Bella had an idea. If she were a toad too, she would

not be afraid anymore. So, she began experimenting with magical potions to transform herself. Eventually, she succeeded.

Now, transformed into a toad, Bella could hop around the garden. She even introduced herself to the toad she had been so afraid of. He told her his name was Tody—and he turned out to be very kind and gentle.

One morning, Bella saw a snake slithering through the forest and hissing. Bella leapt away and hid in her home. Her fear had returned and she was too scared to leave.

What if the snake hurt her? What could she do?

Bella returned to her laboratory, created a new magical potion, and transformed into a beautiful snake. Now she could slide through the entire forest. She became friends with the snake, who was called Serpa and told funny jokes.

But something still worried Bella. What would she need to change into next? Would she ever feel safe?

Sad, alone, and defeated, Bella retreated back into her home.

It was on one of Bella's rare outings that she met Fred, a beautiful butterfly with blue wings. Crying, she told him her story. Then Fred said something that changed Bella.

"We don't have to try to destroy fear. It's there to protect us. What we need is the courage to put fear in its place."

Thoughtful, Bella returned to her laboratory. She looked at all the potions she had created and understood something important: every time she tried to become a different animal, fear changed its shape—but it never disappeared.

Carefully, she took the last potion she would ever make and transformed back into herself: a butterfly.

When she stepped outside, Bella felt fear again. It was still there. But this time she did not run. She opened her wings slowly and, her heart beating fast, she began to fly.

And that is how Bella discovered something essential: trying to be something else did not make her braver.

True courage was when she chose to be herself.

Bella's garden was bigger now that it was full of new friends: Tody, Serpa, and Fred. And Bella was braver too. She never stopped flying again.

3.7.3 A Sensitive Moment: What We Say While a Child Sleeps

The words we say to our children while they are awake deeply shape the way they perceive themselves and face the world. However, there is another especially sensitive period: the time when the child is asleep.

During sleep, the nervous system is more relaxed and emotional defenses are lower. In that climate of calm, words are not experienced as demands or corrections, but as internal experiences of safety and companionship.

As a result of this open and calm state, the time surrounding sleep can become an emotional support space, reinforcing protection, trust, and capacity in the face of what scares the child.

This kind of support allows the child to be able to move through fear while feeling capable—and held.

3.7.4 A Brief Guide to Practice (Orientation Only)

1.   Wait until the child is deeply asleep. REM (rapid eye movement) sleep typically occurs after a period of rest, about one hour after falling asleep. Try to wait at least that long.

2.   Read a short text or speak a phrase related to the fear the child is going through. Use a soft, calm voice, without waking them, repeating the phrase slowly about six times.

3.   Repeat this practice for 21 days. Repetition—when it happens within the context of a calm environment and a secure bond—helps the message integrate deeply and progressively.

The more a positive emotional experience is repeated, the more it consolidates. That is why this practice should not be left out. Through it, you help your child develop courage. If you do not know which phrase to use, here are a few examples.

- **To reinforce courage**: (child's name), you are safe and protected. Your intelligence and your sensitivity live within you.
- **To reinforce love and belonging**: (Child's name), we love you deeply. You are a very important part of our family, and you hold a special place in our hearts.

This is one practice that can be used to support a child. However, the most essential practice of all is helping them experience love and belonging within the family. Feeling loved, welcomed, and emotionally included is what prevents fear from organizing life like a prison.

Love, however, must always be accompanied by respect for autonomy. Children need freedom to make mistakes, take risks, and learn through experience. Love must never be confused with overprotection, because excessive control can trap a child in a world ruled by fear and unnecessary rules.

Overprotection—even when born of good intentions—often limits the development of autonomy and can lead to dependent, insecure adults. That is why it is important to reflect honestly on whether the protection we offer is supporting a child's growth—or silently restricting it.

These dynamics are not expressed only in the individual relationship between adult and child, but also in how bonds organize within the family system. If you have more than one child, these aspects require even more attention. In this context, one essential aspect deserves focus: the lived experience of emotional fairness.

It is common for siblings to complain that they are not the "favorite." In many cases, parents sincerely strive not to show preferences and still jealousy arises—especially when unequal treatment is perceived, even unconsciously. When a child feels they must compete for love or attention, a constant inner tension settles in, not always expressible directly.

In these cases, fear can become a silent pathway for emotional expression. Not because jealousy automatically creates a phobia, but because the experience of insecurity, comparison, or threat to the bond can predispose the child to seek, through fear, a form of protection or recognition. When fairness is truly lived, jealousy loses force and the child can feel loved without comparison—reducing the need for fear to serve that function.

To conclude, it is important to remember that the development of a phobia may—or may not—be related to childhood experiences. If someone reaches adulthood with an intense fear, facing it becomes their responsibility, not their parents' or caregivers'. They did what they could with the resources and awareness they had at that time.

This perspective helps release guilt and opens space for a deeper exploration of fear.

3.7.5 An Insight into the Mind

It is essential to observe how the mind works. The human mind is organized into different levels: conscious, subconscious, and unconscious.

The Conscious Mind
- Reasoning
- Motivation for action
- Short-term memory
- Analysis and decision-making

The Subconscious Mind
- Long-term memory
- Emotions
- Self-preservation instinct
- Habits
- Automatic functions

The Unconscious Mind
- Autonomic nervous system
- Immune system

When we consider these levels, an immediate association often arises: phobias tend to be linked to the domain of the self-preservation instinct, located in the subconscious level. After all, a phobia is a fear reaction. And fear, in its original function, exists to protect us.

The problem appears when the subconscious interprets a signal as dangerous when no real danger exists. In that moment, the body reacts before thought can intervene. There is no time to analyze, question, or relativize: the response is already underway.

For this reason, phobias are not transformed only through willpower or logical reasoning. Fear does not wait for a conscious decision to appear; it emerges as an automatic response—then gets explained, justified, or reinforced by thought.

In childhood, this process takes on a particular weight, because the child does not yet have internal resources to understand or regulate those automatic responses alone. At that stage, the relational environment becomes decisive.

That is why this understanding becomes especially relevant

when we think about children. They do not need parents free of fear—they need adults willing to look at their own fear with honesty. When adults model curiosity instead of avoidance, and presence instead of control, they help a child organize their inner experience.

And it is precisely in that early relational learning—often silent—that the emotional profile begins to form, the same profile that later can sustain a phobia.

When we look at profile and family systems, phobia stops seeming like a bodily whim and reveals its logic: a way of organizing safety when, inside, there is not enough margin.

Understanding this weave—biological, emotional, and relational—does not aim to assign blame. It aims to give fear a place that is smaller than life.

From here on, the focus shifts: from not only understanding what sustains phobia, to beginning to dismantle—carefully and methodically—the circuit that keeps it alive.

4.
FACING CHALLENGES THROUGH THE COURAGE TECHNIQUE

The mere idea of facing a fear often triggers anxiety and, at times, makes the threat feel bigger in the mind. Thoughts appear such as: "I can't," "What if I get overwhelmed?," "If I couldn't do it before, why would I be able to now?" The key is not "to stop feeling," but to learn to hold what you feel with courage. And that can be trained.

Courage is often associated with people who seem confident, brave, independent, and grounded in strong self-esteem. But were they always that way? Probably not. Courage is not a trait we are born with, but a quality we build. The greater the commitment to developing it, the stronger it becomes.

For this reason, I created an acrostic that will help you

cultivate courage. We will bring each letter of the word COURAGE to life in an unusual way, so that you can access a strength you may not have known existed in you—and learn to relate differently to your fears, including phobias, when they arise.

In my clinical practice, I always make it clear that treatment is a collaborative process. Just as I commit to accompanying the person, the initiative for change also needs to come from within the patient. And now, from you.

"When I question why the fear arose and have the courage and audacity to move forward, I discover myself and grow stronger." — Dolores Macioski

4.1 The Elephant Metaphor

Some time ago, I read a metaphor by an unknown author and, before presenting the COURAGE acrostic, I want to invite you to reflect on it. As you read, try to picture the scene.

Have you ever watched an elephant in the circus? During the show, that enormous animal displays astonishing strength. Yet before stepping into the ring, it remains tied—still, contained, held only by a chain that fastens one of its legs to a small stake driven into the ground.

The stake is nothing more than a piece of wood. And although the chain might look strong, it is obvious that an elephant—an animal capable of knocking down a tree by sheer force—could easily free itself by pulling.

So, the question arises: why does it not escape?

Over time, I found out—fortunately, someone was curious enough to discover the answer—that the circus elephant does not run away because it was tied to that stake when it was very small. I close my eyes and imagine the newborn elephant, tied up, pulling with all its strength to break free. But despite its effort, it can't. The stake is too strong for it at that moment.

The little elephant tries again and again. Until, exhausted, it accepts its fate: to remain tied, swaying its body from side to side, waiting for the moment it will go on stage.

And so, when the elephant grows, it no longer tries to break the chain. Not because it lacks the strength, but because it believes it cannot. For it to finally free itself, something extraordinary would have to happen—like a fire. The fear of flames could drive it, desperately, to snap the chain and run.

And then the reflection emerges: Is your fear the result of a situation you could not resolve in the past—perhaps in childhood? Like that elephant tied up from a very young age, it is possible that you have become so bound to your fears that you have come to believe you are incapable of freeing yourself from them. And yet, through self-knowledge, you can discover the true extent of your strength.

Then something becomes unmistakably clear: a truth that was always there, but that you may never have seen with sharpness. You are far greater than your fears.

With that reflection in mind, I invite you to discover how each letter of the word COURAGE can bring you closer to your goal of facing fear—in all its forms, using the strength that already exists within you.

4.2 COURAGE

C: Confidence in Yourself

Confidence in yourself does not appear overnight; it is built through the way you perceive yourself and the way you treat yourself internally. Have you ever paused to consider what self-esteem truly is?

Self-esteem rests on two pillars: self-efficacy (what I feel I am capable of doing) and self-perception (how I see myself and how I treat myself). When both are strengthened, a more stable confidence is born: self-confidence.

Healthy self-esteem leads to inner peace and harmony, eliminating the need for constant comparison or competition with others. It also means neither overvaluing yourself nor undervaluing others, but recognizing your own limits and abilities with clarity.[1]

But for self-esteem to be solid and translate into self-confidence, self-knowledge is essential. After all, is it possible to trust what is unknown? It is through self-knowledge that a person develops the ability to value themselves and strengthen their self-image.

What is your self-image? When you think of yourself, what is the first thing that comes to mind?

The answers to these questions offer clear clues about the state of your self-esteem. If the image that emerges highlights mainly flaws and pushes positive qualities into the background, it is worth pausing: it is an invitation to go deeper into self-knowledge.

Many times, self-esteem does not need more effort, but more structure. Organizing who we are—without judgment—is a form of inner care.

In addition to being a psychologist, I am also a business administrator. This dual training allows me to adapt practical tools to the emotional reality in which they must be applied. That is how I began using part of the SWOT analysis (Strengths, Weaknesses, Opportunities, Threats) to help strengthen self-esteem through self-knowledge.

In the business world, this analysis aims to identify an organization's central points, offering a global view that makes strategic decision-making easier. Philip Kotler notes that after applying SWOT analysis, a company becomes able to define goals and plan with greater clarity.[2] In a similar way, when we use this tool on a personal level, we can know ourselves more deeply and visualize clearer paths to develop confidence in ourselves.

For this exercise, I suggest we focus only on two parts of the analysis: strengths and weaknesses. Take a moment to answer the following.

- **What are my strengths?** (What qualities do I recognize in myself?)
- **What are my weaknesses?** (What can I develop or strengthen?)

Recognizing your own qualities is not always easy, because many people learned to look at themselves through lack rather than through value. This exercise is not meant to inflate self-esteem, but to rebalance the gaze each person directs toward themselves.

By looking at strengths, we do not deny weaknesses. What changes is their place in the mind. When attention fixes exclusively on what is missing, limitations grow and take center stage. When perspective widens, weaknesses stop occupying the entire scene and can be worked on without harshness or self-attack.

It is in that inner reordering that bravery begins to be built: not as the absence of fragility, but as a fairer relationship with who you are.

Self-image → Self-esteem → Self-confidence = Courage

When we understand this cycle, we see the interdependence among its elements. If self-image is fragile, the entire chain suffers. And then an inevitable question arises: where could courage come from?

That is why the final link before courage, within this process, is self-confidence. But it is not enough to "believe in yourself"; it is necessary to develop real, sustained confidence in your own capacity.

Among the books I recommend is *Fear Is Mental Masturbation*, by Giulio Cesare Giacobbe, which I consider especially relevant. In this work, the author expresses a view similar to mine: for him, three forces make us adults—self-esteem, emotional independence, and the joy of living.[3]

From my perspective, these three forces are essential for those who want to face their fears with courage, because doing so requires emotional maturity. That is why, in the letter O of our acronym, we will learn the importance of developing independence.

Confidence to Change

From the earliest moments of human history, movement

and adaptation were essential for survival. Change was not a choice—it was a natural response to life's demands.

Over time, however, human beings began to settle, building personal and collective roots. Those roots offered stability and a sense of belonging, but they also made it harder to leave the familiar behind. Civilizations emerged—with all their advances and their limitations.

Today, many people remain emotionally anchored to what they know. That attachment often feels protective and reasonable, yet it can quietly turn into stagnation. Physical change may no longer be a direct condition for survival, but emotional change remains indispensable for growth.

Resistance to change is rarely about laziness or lack of desire. More often, it reflects fragile self-confidence. When confidence in our own abilities is low, the unknown feels threatening, and staying where we are seems safer.

True change is not merely an act of courage; it is an expression of self-confidence. It is the quiet recognition that even without certainty, we can face challenges, tolerate discomfort, and hold ourselves steady throughout the process.

When someone becomes rigid in the face of necessary transformation, they are not protecting themselves—they are postponing emotional maturity. In this sense, change is not a loss, but a movement toward authorship of one's own life.

That is why independence occupies a central place in the next stage of this journey—not as distance or isolation, but as the capacity to stand emotionally on one's own two feet, with responsibility, flexibility, and confidence.

O: Obtain Emotional Independence

Emotional independence does not arise spontaneously; it is the result of psychological maturation. At the beginning of life, human vulnerability requires dependence: care, protection, and external support. Growing up means gradually moving from that primary dependence toward the ability to internally sustain what once needed to be regulated by others.

When we recognize our strengths, as we did in the previous exercise, we build self-confidence. That confidence strengthens autonomy and progressively loosens the grip of emotional dependence. Still, this process is neither simple nor automatic. To understand emotional independence, we must return to the very origin of dependence.

When Fear Organizes the Bond

It is precisely when this developmental movement is not completed that certain symptoms begin to take the place of emotional support.

In clinical practice, many phobias persist not because danger is real, but because the symptom has become an unconscious bond. In these cases, fear is not only a response to risk—it becomes a strategy for preserving belonging. When early fears, unmet needs, or emotional wounds have not been processed, they remain active in the present and shape adult life.

For this reason, emotional independence can feel less like freedom and more like abandonment. Letting go of fear may be unconsciously experienced as separation, betrayal, or loss—as if courage meant breaking a silent emotional contract. In such cases, the phobia does not resist treatment; it resists loss. Understanding this kind of resistance requires widening our view to the early roots of the psyche.

From the Inner Child to the Emotional Adult

Sigmund Freud emphasized the importance of childhood analysis in understanding symptoms—not only what we consciously remember, but especially what belongs to "forgotten childhood," where unresolved emotional experiences remain hidden.[4] For Freud, so-called childhood neurosis is not confined to the past; it is a set of early fears, bonds, and reactions that can remain active in adulthood when they have not been worked through. Childhood neurosis manifests in adult life whenever imaginary fears continue to organize behavior.[5]

Imaginary fears are characteristic of childhood. But when they persist into adulthood—even when external reality no longer justifies them—they reveal that the person is still responding through a childish emotional logic. Someone can function competently in many areas and still react emotionally like a child seeking protection.

In childhood neurosis, fear does not serve only a defensive function in the face of danger; it also organizes the bond. Fear can guarantee presence, care, and closeness. When this logic is not reworked in adulthood, fear stops being a developmental stage and may crystallize into a phobia. A phobia, then, does not express only fear; it expresses the difficulty of sustaining emotional autonomy without losing the internal bond that once provided security.

This conflict often appears in profiles marked by self-imposed pressure, a need for control, and difficulty tolerating uncertainty. These are not signs of weakness, but the result of constant tension between an inner child seeking protection and an adult trying to uphold responsibility. Sometimes, this child was shaped by early experiences of comparison—feeling less cared for than a sibling, for example—and developed the need to secure the other's presence through dependence or control.

In adulthood, that same logic can return as fear, avoidance, or phobia.

Giacobbe's ideas are relevant here as well. He links childhood neurosis to dependence on parents or caregivers. That dependence does not simply dissolve when an adult leaves home; in many cases, it is not overcome, but displaced onto a partner or other significant figures—repeating the same primary emotional pattern.

The metaphor of the monster under the bed helps clarify this dynamic. For a child, the fear is entirely real. No explanation eliminates it instantly. Only through experience—growing, testing reality, and developing internal resources—does that fear lose its power.

The same is true of phobias in adulthood. When fear remains imaginary yet emotionally convincing, it suggests that the inner child is still organizing the response. Emotional independence begins when the adult recognizes this dynamic, understands how fear has become redundant, and takes responsibility for facing it—without delegating that emotional task to others.

Emotional independence, therefore, is not isolation, coldness, or emotional distance. It is the ability to stand emotionally on one's own two feet—tolerating discomfort, making decisions, and navigating uncertainty without surrendering authorship of one's own life.

As this independence develops, fear gradually loses its organizing function. What once "protected" by limiting begins to make room for growth. And from this position—firm, mature, and self-referential—the person can sustain themselves emotionally without using fear as a guide.

Where the child waited for someone else to choose them, the adult learns to choose themselves. That is emotional independence: no longer seeking from others the confirmation of what can already be born within. When the source of courage is no longer external, fear loses its function—and courage finally finds somewhere to live.

However, for this inner choice to be possible, it is necessary to understand which emotion most often stands in the way: anguish. Many times, it is not fear itself that paralyzes us, but the anguish hidden beneath it. Where the child once feared losing love, care, or presence, the adult continues to react as if that loss were still imminent. That is why exploring the origin of anguish is an essential step toward gaining emotional independence.

What Is Anguish?

Anguish is a displaced emotion that can lead to phobia. When I speak of anguish, I am referring to a set of primary emotions—such as helplessness, loneliness, frustration, or the fear of losing love—that leave a deep imprint and, often, become displaced into fear. Although they may take different forms, they all share the same root: the lived experience of lack.

At its core, anguish is an experience of emotional deprivation: something essential was taken from us or withheld, generating momentary frustration and a persistent unease. Whether it is affection, love, a person, or a condition, losing something can leave us in anguish—even when we are not fully aware of it.

Understanding our fears requires entering our existential cave, searching for clues that allow us to unravel the origin of that anguish. Fear often conceals far more than we imagine.

Some people feel anguish because they cannot respond in moments of discomfort—especially those who struggle to express what they feel. Others are so "withdrawn" in their actions that suffering in silence seems like a possible way out. And there are also those who, at some point in life, felt abandoned or neglected and still struggle to hold that wound today.

These seemingly ordinary experiences can activate profound states of anguish precisely because they confront the individual with what they have not been able to process.

That is why, for those who suffer from phobias, fear can function as a shield against anguish: a kind of watchtower that prevents this deeper emotion from moving into the foreground.[6]

Let us look at some practical examples to understand this more clearly.

Example 1: Fear of Elevators

One patient had a deep fear of elevators. Just imagining the numbers rising—floor after floor—was enough to overwhelm her. Ascending in an elevator was her greatest terror.

As we explored the origin of this fear, we found a powerful analogy beneath the phobia. Unconsciously, she feared growing up. Her parents had overprotected her in childhood, which paradoxically deprived her of independence. Growing up becomes difficult when you have lived under excessive protection.

Without realizing it, watching the numbers climb on the elevator panel triggered the anxiety associated with growing up: the sense of losing protection, being left without support, and not knowing whether she would be able to sustain herself. Her fear of "falling" was, in truth, fear of becoming independent.

In her case, the phobia acted as a shield. Fear of elevators prevented contact with her deepest anxiety—the anxiety of leaving behind her place as a protected child. Treatment needed to address the elevator fear, but it was equally crucial for her to understand that growing up did not mean falling; it meant becoming free.

Example 2: Fear of Heights

Another patient feared heights. She loved playing tennis and was highly skilled, but she consistently failed at volleys (hitting the ball before it touches the ground). Why? Unconsciously, that movement resembled approaching someone emotionally—opening up.

Because she struggled to express feelings, she avoided that gesture. What she could not face relationally—emotional exposure, the possibility of being seen or rejected—shifted into anxiety. With no direct outlet, that anxiety was displaced into fear of heights, as if openness and exposure made her vulnerable and likely to fall.

In her case, the phobia functioned as a defense. Fear of

heights protected her from encountering a deeper anxiety: the anxiety of becoming emotionally available and therefore vulnerable to not being accepted.

Example 3: Fear of Driving

A very common case among my patients is a driving phobia. Many report a deep fear of responsibility—not only for their own safety, but also for those around them. It is natural to feel some weight when learning to drive. But when that fear becomes paralyzing, there is usually anxiety lurking underneath.

What comes to mind when we think of driving? For most people, the answer is freedom: going wherever you want, whenever you want, listening to your favorite music. It sounds wonderful. But freedom can feel terrifying when anxiety has been displaced.

For many, driving evokes not only the practical act of operating a car, but also the symbolic demand to navigate life alone.

For those who experienced abandonment, loneliness, or neglect early in life, this "freedom" triggers anxiety about having no support—the childlike feeling of having no one to turn to.

That is why, even in adulthood, many patients do not feel capable of driving. Freedom does not only expose them to the road; it exposes them to themselves. It awakens the anxiety of acting independently, taking charge, and assuming responsibility for one's own decisions.

In this case, the phobia protects them from a deeper experience: feeling alone in the world.

I could list many more examples of displaced anxiety, because it is a common dynamic in phobias. Behind each intense fear there is often an older, deeper emotion—one the child could not name, and the adult still tries to avoid.

The core point is this: to free yourself from fear, you must become independent—even from the anxieties that have bound you to a mistaken belief. When you stop running from anxiety and begin to understand it, fear loses its function. And it is there, in the space where autonomy replaces imaginary protection, that courage can finally live.

U: Uncover Meaning, and the Joy of Being Alive

People fear death so deeply that, without realizing it, they end up not living. That is why, to understand courage, it is essential to look directly at the fear of dying—not because we should obsess over it, but because facing it returns us to life.

Death is the one certainty we all share. Sooner or later, each of us will have to face it. The unknown surrounding it stirs unease: no one can say with absolute certainty what happens afterward. It is true that many people report near-death experiences—intense, transformative moments filled with light or clarity—but even those accounts cannot be treated as proof. And when something remains wrapped in mystery, the mind tends to fill the unknown void with whatever it is feeling: fantasy, anguish, or avoidance.

And sometimes that same search for meaning turns toward life. Because what disturbs us is not always death in itself, but the feeling that something essential—a relationship we did not care for properly, a dream we postponed, a truth we did not dare to speak—has been left on hold. The mind interprets that "unfinishedness" as a threat, because what remains unresolved often weighs more than what is already lost.

We do not all react to death in the same way. Some of us accept this reality with serenity; others develop intense anxiety. Those who suffer from anxiety disorders often interpret any bodily signal as danger. In obsessive-compulsive disorder, for instance, a person may wash their hands compulsively out of fear of getting sick or dying; in panic disorder, a simple palpitation can feel like an imminent heart attack. And in many phobias, fear of flying, elevators, heights, or blood can conceal—without the person realizing it—an even deeper fear: the possibility of death.

Yet this reaction does not arise in a vacuum. In the present, we are all in the same position: no one knows how much time they have left. The difference is not in the number of days, but in how we inhabit them. Some cultures, such as Mexican, transform death into celebration: a festival full of color, music, food, and memory. In many families, children are not taught that death is a taboo topic—because it is part of a tradition that honors life through remembrance.

In many modern Western societies, however, death is covered in silence—and what is not spoken often turn into fear. That absence of words and meaning leaves us without tools to relate to what is inevitable.

As researcher Norma Van Rooy writes, "like a child at birth, we have no choice but to surrender to the unknown."

And it is precisely that unknown—when it is not named or thought about—that opens space for anguish. It is not death itself that hurts most, but the lack of language with which to approach it. When a topic becomes unnameable, the mind fills it with fantasies, fears, and distortions. Speaking about death does not bring it closer. It makes it more comprehensible.

When we accept this truth, something inside us reorganizes: we begin to live with more attention, more tenderness, more purpose. For Buddhists, a certain level of detachment is essential not only to die well, but to live well. Accepting impermanence does not pull us away from daily life, it invites us back into it—through the smallest gestures.

Think for a moment: why do you save your best dishes for a special occasion? Why does that wine you love always "wait for another day?" What if the special day was today—and you simply did not know it?

Reflecting on death is not meant to darken your perspective, but to clarify it. Because when we understand time is limited, we also discover we have the power—and the responsibility—to choose how we want to live it.

And here is a fundamental clinical truth: for those who live with anxiety or phobias, fear of dying often hides an even greater fear—the fear of living fully. Living requires risk. Decisions. Responsibility. Openness to connection. Tolerance for uncertainty. And that can feel as threatening as death itself.

So, if you experience anxiety symptoms and want to free yourself from fear, you will need to gradually expose yourself to life—its challenges and its possibilities. As life opens, even slightly, motivation begins to find room to rise.

And this brings us to the heart of this section: the fear of dying begins to lose strength when we find a reason to live.

That statement is not only philosophical; it is also

supported by research. Studies by Sheldon Solomon, Jeff Greenberg, and Tom Pyszczynski—creators of Terror Management Theory—have shown that people who live with greater meaning, purpose, or connection to values tend to experience significantly less death anxiety.[7] When life fills with meaning, death stops feeling like a constant threat and becomes integrated into the human experience.

This becomes evident in clinical work. Think, for example, of Livia. From childhood, she had a special sensitivity with children: she could calm them, understand them, make them feel seen. But every goodbye tightened something in her chest. That repeated sadness led her to question why. Over time, she realized her sensitivity came from her own story: she had grown up in an unstable home, where affection was scarce and separation frequent. What had once been a wound became a compass. Today, as a social worker, she supports children who need stability and love.

Her purpose was born in the same place where fear used to live—confirming what psychological research has shown: when life gains meaning, fear loses some of its power. The strength that now supports so many children was forged in the adversity she herself had to survive.

Just as Livia turned her wound into purpose, you can also discover where your strength comes from. To support you in this process, here is a practical guide I use with my patients— simple, yet deeply revealing.

When you complete this guide with honesty, you will discover something essential: your purpose does not arise *despite* your wounds—it emerges *from* them.

SKILLS (What are you naturally good at?)	PASSIONS (What do you deeply enjoy doing?)
Examples Cooking, caring for children, and communicating.	**Examples** Eating, reading, playing with children.
IDEAL (What is your mission? Why are you here?)	**SELF-IMPROVEMENT** (Where does your strength come from? What wound became your driving force?)
Example Helping children find homes where they can grow up with love and support.	**Example** I grew up in an environment that was not healthy for a child.

Motivation—that inner sense that guides, sustains, and ignites you—does not erase fear, but it makes fear smaller in comparison to what truly matters. Where there was paralysis, direction begins to form. Where there was threat, life returns.

And it is precisely from this place of purpose that we can move toward the most practical steps of treatment.

After recognizing the strength that lives in you—and the

meaning that moves you—one decisive step remains: exposure, the very heart of change.

R: Relax and Breathe

Now that you understand the importance of self-confidence and emotional independence, we move to the R in our COURAGE acrostic. Here, we will explore—practically— how relaxation and breathing can shift you from anxiety into calm.

Peveler and Johnston (1976) found that relaxation can increase access to positive information in memory, making it easier to find alternatives to danger-focused thoughts.[8]

There are many different breathing and relaxation techniques. Here we will focus on diaphragmatic (abdominal) breathing and progressive muscle relaxation—both widely used for decades in the treatment of anxiety disorders and in stress management.

I have adapted these two exercises based on clinical experience, so they are simple, practical, and accessible.

Diaphragmatic Breathing

We tend to breathe in a shallow, rapid way, which can lead to what is known as hyperventilation—usually in response to anxiety, stress, or panic. In this state, the lungs expel carbon dioxide too quickly, which can contribute to several physical symptoms associated with anxiety, such as sweating, palpitations, and dizziness.

With diaphragmatic breathing, it is possible to slow the breathing rate, support a steadier breathing pattern, and reduce physical activation. This type of breathing happens naturally and can be easily observed in babies, whose abdomen moves more than their chest when they breathe.

If at any point you feel dizzy or uncomfortable, return to your natural breathing rhythm and resume the exercise later.

Exercise

Now, let us practice a breathing exercise. Before you begin, sit in a comfortable position, with your body relaxed. We will practice diaphragmatic breathing. In this technique, the abdomen expands as air comes in and contracts as it goes out; the chest barely moves. During inhalation, the diaphragm contracts, and during exhalation, the muscle relaxes.

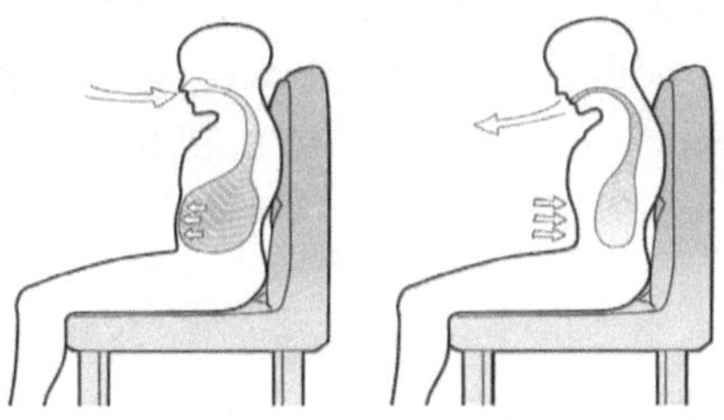

Place one hand on your abdomen and the other on your chest. Inhale slowly and deeply through your nose, counting to **three** in your mind. Hold the air for **three** seconds. Then exhale slowly through your mouth, counting to **six**. Emphasize the exhale with a long "aaaah," keeping your mouth open and relaxed. Let tension leave your body with each exhalation.

Do it once more. As you inhale, remember that peace, safety, and protection are entering you. As you exhale, let fears, insecurities, anxiety, and anything that worries you leave your mind and your heart.

Progressive Muscle Relaxation

The progressive muscle relaxation technique is used to induce neuromuscular relaxation. Muscle tension is one of the main components of anxiety, and it appears automatically and involuntarily.

This technique promotes control over voluntary muscles in order to reach a state of relaxation, allowing you to tense and then relax the main muscle groups of the body, one at a time.

By alternating between tension and relaxation, you learn to distinguish both states and develop greater awareness of the areas of your body that tend to hold tension.

Exercise

Now, let us do an exercise that will allow you to fully relax the muscles of your body. Before you begin, find a comfortable position and breathe deeply and calmly for a few moments. Rest your arms on your legs and keep your legs slightly apart.

Remember that this technique will help you relax and stay calm when you face challenging situations. Notice the difference in your body when it is tense—and then when it is relaxed.

Now, tense each muscle group. Following the instructions, we will hold the tension for about **ten** seconds before releasing it, allowing a rest of about **twenty** seconds between each muscle group.

Let us begin. Keep your body relaxed. Direct your attention to the muscles in your arms and hands. Make a moderate fist with your right hand. Bend your arm toward your shoulder, keeping your fingers pointing toward your body. Tighten more firmly for **ten** seconds.

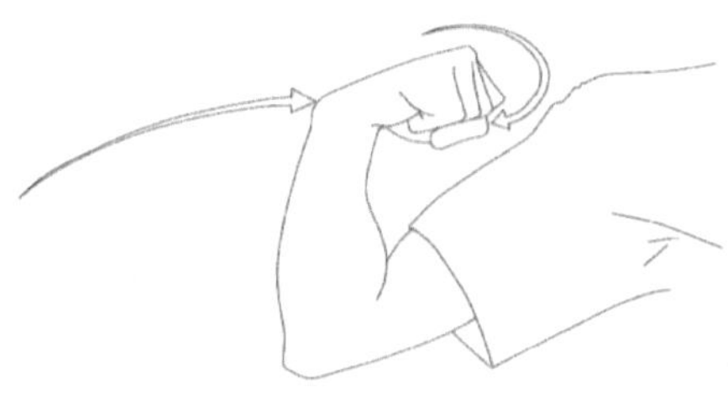

Make a moderate fist with your left hand. Bend your arm toward your shoulder, keeping your fingers pointing toward your body. Tighten more firmly for **ten** seconds. Feel the tension in the muscles of your arm and then release, letting your hand return to its relaxed resting position. Keep the rest of your body loose and relaxed.

Now, bring your attention to your right leg and foot. Try to keep the rest of your body relaxed. Then lift your right leg off the floor until it is fully extended in front of you. Pull your toes toward you and tense the entire leg as much as you can. Notice the contraction in your foot, calf, knee, and thigh. Tighten and hold the tension for **ten** seconds, and then gradually relax—lowering your leg and bending your knee slightly until your foot rests on the floor.

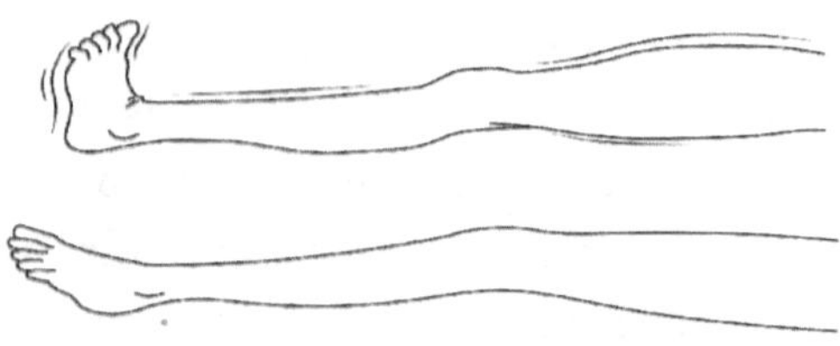

Lift your left leg and foot off the floor, extending them fully in front of you. Pull your toes toward you and tense the entire leg as much as possible. Feel the tension in your foot, calf, knee, and thigh. Tighten and hold the tension for **ten** seconds and then gradually relax—lowering your leg and bending your knee slightly until your foot rests on the floor.

Now bring your attention to the muscles in both legs and feet. Tighten and hold for ten seconds, and then release completely, letting go of all tension. Relax the muscles of your legs and feet fully. Feel the difference between when they were tense and contracted and now, as they become looser and more relaxed.

In this moment, pay attention to your breathing. Tense your chest by taking a deep inhalation. Hold the air, count to **three**, exhale, and release.

Now tense your abdomen by drawing the muscles inward toward your spine. Tighten and hold for **ten** seconds, and then release slowly.

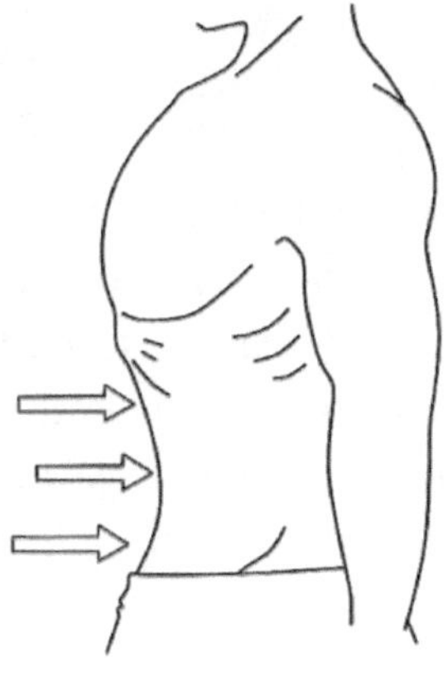

You may notice a growing sense of calm and ease as you gradually bring your attention to your shoulders, keeping your whole body relaxed. Lift your shoulders up toward your ears, breathing calmly, and feel all the tension stored there for **ten** seconds. Release and let all the tension go completely— along with any anxiety that was being held in these muscles. Relax your shoulder muscles.

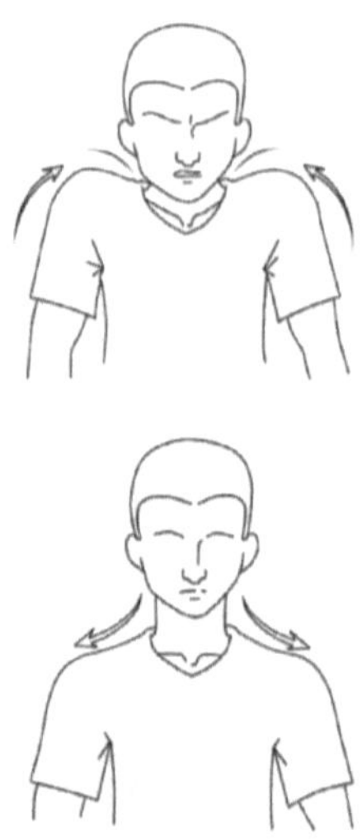

Now let us move to the facial muscles. Bring your attention to your face. Furrow your brow as if you were worried. Hold that position for about **ten** seconds. Notice the tension building in your forehead. Relax and release your forehead completely, and observe how it feels as the muscles soften and become looser and more relaxed.

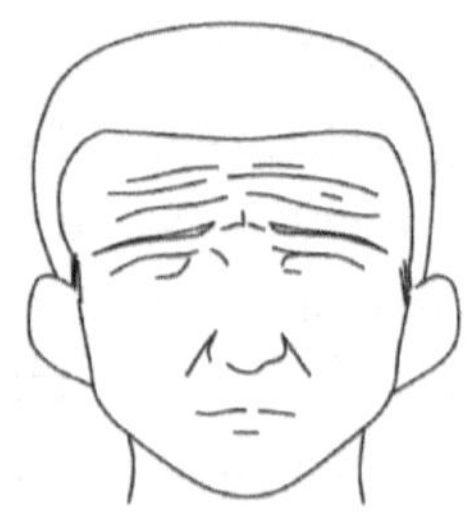

Now make a big, forced smile. Stretch the muscles in your cheeks, pulling the corners of your mouth back. Hold that tension—firmly—for **ten** seconds. Now relax your muscles. Let your whole body rest at ease and and keep breathing calmly.

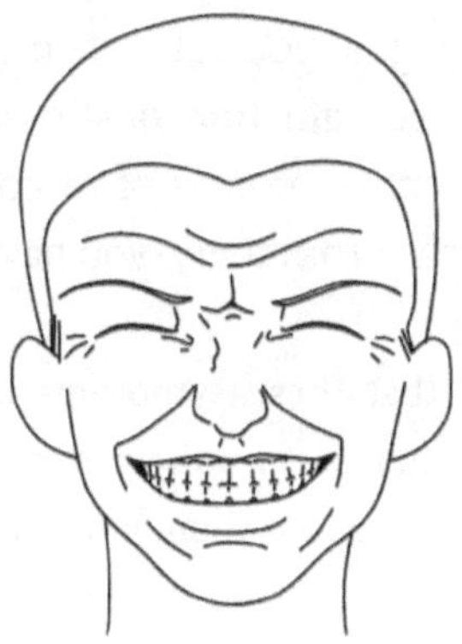

All the muscles in your body are relaxed—loose and soft. Your body is calm and at ease. Allow yourself to sink into the deep sense of well-being that now fills your whole being.

A: Accept Your Physical Symptoms

Yes—you need to accept the physical symptoms of fear. And to do that, it is essential to understand that they are normal. The first step to facing fear with courage is *acceptance*.

If your heart races before your wedding.
If you feel palpitations before a trip.
If your hands sweat when you see a dog approaching.
These symptoms are normal.

What would be unusual is feeling nothing at all.

When you face a fear, experiencing the body's anxiety response is a natural process—one your body will not simply stop doing. So, it is better to stop treating it as a problem and start treating it as a signal you can ride out.

When a phobic object, situation, or stimulus triggers you, you will go through the entire process of reactions and symptoms discussed in Chapter 2. From there, you have two options.

1.   Understand that these symptoms are normal and that they will pass—until they fade on their own.

2.   Worry intensely about them and make them grow stronger and stronger.

Which option sounds more sensible? If you want to regain control of the situation, you will obviously choose the first. You need to understand that every time you amplify a symptom, you intensify it.

Anxiety → physical symptoms → anxiety → physical symptoms

Anxiety creates symptoms you know very well. In turn, those symptoms can generate even more anxiety—leading to more symptoms (or symptoms that feel even stronger). That is why you need to break this cycle.

Anxiety → physical symptoms → ~~anxiety~~ → ~~physical symptoms~~

When you feel physical symptoms, you need to accept that they will pass. No matter how intense they seem, they will not kill you. You need to understand that. How? By breathing and relaxing—which you practiced in the previous section—and, if necessary, saying to yourself (even out loud):

- "These symptoms are normal"
- "I'm going to be okay"
- "I accept what I am feeling."

And yes—you will be okay. Panic symptoms can be intense, but they are not dangerous. The nervous system cannot sustain a peak level of activation for long: it rises, reaches a maximum, and then begins to come down.

When, instead of fighting, you accept what you are feeling and focus on your breathing, you break the feedback loop of anxiety and symptoms—and calm arrives sooner.

From here, the next step is learning how to direct your thoughts—especially automatic ones—so they do not fuel fear.

G: Guide Negative Thoughts Away

In Chapter 2, where you learned about the physiology of fear, we discussed automatic thoughts—and the power they can have over you *if you allow them to.*

Now you need to learn how to guide those thoughts, no matter how intense they may feel when they show up.

The first step is to bring the thought onto rational ground. Remember the prefrontal cortex? You need to put it in charge—by analyzing distorted thoughts so you can replace them. But how?

Before anything else, you need to *pause.*

Pause and assess whether the thoughts are negative and whether they are escalating your anxiety. If you have a fear of flying and you are boarding a plane, what kinds of thoughts might be automatic or distorted?

"This isn't safe."
"This plane is going to crash."
"There are so many airplane accidents."
"It was a mistake to come."
Pause.

Look at those thoughts: do they create more suffering? If the answer is yes, they need to be replaced as soon as possible. Do not wait for them to gain momentum—take the wheel before they take you.

One simple and highly effective way to replace negative thoughts is the "safe place" technique, popularized by Sofia Bauer.[9] As the name suggests, it involves guiding your mind to a safe place—real or imagined—when you are facing anxiety or anguish.

Let us go back to the airplane example. If fear-loaded thoughts arise, you can replace them by bringing up a safe place: a spot where you played as a child, a meaningful trip, or a calming scene you create in your imagination. So, in summary, if negative thoughts show up you must do the following.

1. **Pause**: If needed, use a breathing technique.

2. **Bring your mind back to reason**: Is this thought realistic – or is it fear talking?

3. **Journey to a safe place**: A positive memory, a landscape, a corner of the mind that brings you calm.

These three steps can restore control over your mind—and, as a result, over your emotions and your symptoms, including physical ones.

Another technique I often recommend to my patients is the rubber band method. The idea is simple: wear a rubber band on your wrist, especially when you know you are going to face something that triggers fear. When the phobic situation appears, gently pull the band and release it. Why?

That small sensation on the skin is not meant to hurt. It is meant to remind you to take control back. The physical cue interrupts the negative thought stream and helps you bring the moment back to rational ground. Simple—and effective.

There are also techniques tailored to specific phobias, such as the airsickness-bag exercise, which I suggest to patients with fear of flying. This involves writing negative thoughts on the vomit bag found in the airplane seat pocket. And then? You throw it away at the end of the session—just as you should do with the thoughts that pile up in your mind. The physical act of discarding them sends a clear message: you can let them go.

You can also shift your focus by observing your surroundings—colors, shapes, sizes. Choose one object and explore it in detail. If your attention drifts, bring it back. This technique helps interrupt the fear cycle in real time.

Another powerful way to disarm negative thoughts is gratitude. Focusing on what you have, instead of what is missing, promotes well-being, calm, and a sense of abundance.

Tomorrow we may not have the same good fortune we have today: a home, loved ones, the health to practice a sport. That is why gratitude belongs in the present. Keeping a gratitude journal can help you build this habit: every day, write down something you are grateful for—big or small. Returning to those notes when negative thoughts arise is an effective way to replace them.

This reminds me of a classic book, *Pollyanna*, by Eleanor H. Porter. The protagonist faces situations that would destabilize any child, yet she chooses to look for the positive—and to let that perspective guide her life. That is how she overcomes adversity.

I could share many other ways to handle negative thoughts, but they are all variations of the same process: **pause, rationalize, replace**. So, remember this process and use it whenever you need to regain control of negative thinking.

This becomes even easier when you understand how the brain works.

Your Brain Runs on Associations

The brain is a powerful connection-making machine. But when information it holds is incomplete, the associations it creates do not always serve you. Consider these examples.

What animal comes to mind when someone says "man's best friend?" What color do you think of when I say the word "hope?" You probably thought of a dog and the color green, right? And it happened automatically—without effort—because your brain had enough information to believe those connections made sense.

But not all associations are accurate. Negative thoughts appear suddenly—so you must pause, bring them to reason, and replace them.

When you do that, you teach your brain which associations

are true and which are distortions. And that gives you the courage you need to face your phobias.

E: Establish an Exposure Hierarchy

To face a fear, you first need to understand what stage you are currently at within your phobia. Even two people with the same diagnosis can experience completely different degrees of intensity.

For example, two patients with animal phobia may both fear dogs—yet in opposite ways: one may enter a phobic state simply by seeing a dog across the street, while the other walks calmly if the dog is on a leash but freezes if it is loose. That is why it's essential to identify which stage each person is at before beginning the desensitization process.

Once the severity is clarified, we begin **systematic desensitization**, which was developed by Wolpe.[10] This method involves gradually exposing the patient to the object, being, or situation they fear. The key to its effectiveness is **gradualness**—because in exposure, you do not only desensitize a stimulus: you **rewrite a story**. The brain is not afraid of the needle, the dog, or the height; it is afraid of the meaning it once assigned to those objects and experiences in order to survive. Each level in this hierarchy is a step back toward emotional autonomy—and toward a version of you that no longer needs to run away.

To make this journey more effective, it is helpful to combine exposure with the breathing and relaxation techniques you learned earlier. Think again of video games: no one reaches the final level without completing the first, or all the ones in between. As you progressively expose yourself to the phobic stimulus, it becomes more familiar and less intimidating. This process is called **habituation**: making what once felt threatening feel so ordinary that the brain finally understands it is not truly dangerous.

Technology has also transformed this path. In the past, patients could only imagine the feared stimulus—or confront it physically. Today, thanks to virtual reality (VR), it is possible to see, hear, and *feel* what frightens you in an immersive way, without physical exposure. This tool will be explained in greater depth later, but it has already become an extraordinary ally in the treatment of phobias.

To illustrate how a desensitization hierarchy works, imagine you have a fear of needles or blood. If, in our first session, I asked you to get a blood test, you would likely develop aversion. Instead, we would build a gradual process: first visualizing a lab mentally, then imagining yourself taking a number and answering basic questions at reception, then observing professionals handling tubes and clinical material in the waiting room, later watching a blood draw performed on another person—first a simple puncture, then a more complex one, and finally going through the procedure yourself.

Each hierarchy must be personalized. And here is an essential truth: to learn to manage anxiety, you must allow yourself to feel it without fleeing from it. Anxiety is not overcome by preventing it from appearing; it is overcome by moving through it safely until the brain learns it is not dangerous. If you interrupt the process every time anxiety rises, your mind will never learn that it can hold the sensation and continue forward.

Along this path, bringing in playful elements can be profoundly transformative. Play is not only for children—it is an intelligent, emotionally deep way of working with imagination, creativity, and emotional memory. When we teach a child to write, we use clay, colors, games. Why? Because learning through play is more effective than learning through pressure. And with phobias, the same applies: fear loses rigidity when it enters territory where it does not know how to operate.

Play is a place fear does not know how to enter.

Many patients with arachnophobia, for example, suffer even when they hear the word "spider." Some have nightmares, avoid parks or gardens, and feel tense at the possibility of encountering one. For them, I propose an exercise as simple as it is surprising: playing with a rubber spider—and painting its nails.

It may sound strange, but the foundation is profound: you assign human, harmless, even humorous qualities to what frightens you. A spider worried about its manicure is far less likely to be processed as a predator. Touching it, placing a hat on it, "making it up," drawing it with big eyes, or dressing it in sneakers creates new associations in the brain—safer and kinder than the old ones. Each playful experience replaces, softens, and reworks the feared image.

You can do the same with your own fear: draw it, name it, change its shape, give it accessories, invent a story. The more familiar it becomes, the less power it has over you. Play turns the unknown into something manageable—and what is manageable is no longer terrifying.

This entire process—hierarchy, exposure, habituation, play—leads you to an essential realization: the fear was never as big as it seemed. What was enormous was not the stimulus. It was the distance between you and your own confidence. And now, step by step, you begin to close that distance.

That is real change.

That is the beginning of freedom.

To sustain that path, we revisit the COURAGE technique.

C – Confidence in Yourself
O – Obtain Emotional Independence
U – Uncover Meaning (and the Joy of Being Alive)
R – Relax and Breathe
A – Accept Your Physical Symptoms
G – Guide Negative Thoughts Away
E – Establish an Exposure Hierarchy

Throughout this process, remember to focus on what makes moving forward through life worth it, even with fear.

In the next chapters, you will learn how to integrate the best of technology—which allows safety, gradual exposure, and a sense of control—with real-life exposure, so you can face fear directly and reclaim your freedom.

5.

VIRTUAL REALITY AND THE INTEGRATED TREATMENT OF PHOBIAS

Do you think VR is a recent innovation? In fact, its exploration began almost two centuries ago, which makes it difficult to pinpoint a single origin.

In 1838, the British physicist Sir Charles Wheatstone invented the stereoscope—a device made of rudimentary goggles with two angled lenses. Basic as it may seem today, it produced a sense of immersion by enhancing depth and enlarging images.[1]

Over time, new technologies continued refining this feeling of presence, paving the way for what we now call virtual reality. The 1990s marked a turning point: VR stopped being a laboratory curiosity and became more accessible. Advancements driven by the entertainment industry eventually reached the field of mental health as well.[2]

But what, exactly, is VR? Virtual reality is an immersive experience: it creates a fully digital environment and produces a sense of presence, even though your body remains somewhere else.

5.1 How Virtual Reality "Tricks" the Brain

Yes, virtual and augmented reality (AR) technologies are designed to "trick the brain," but only in the service of treatment.

As we saw in Chapter 2, the fear response activates with remarkable speed. The brain often reacts before it has time to evaluate whether a threat is real. Because the instinct of self-preservation operates largely at a subconscious level, the body responds impulsively, long before conscious reasoning can intervene.

This is why a projected spider can represent, for the brain, a perceived risk similar to a real spider walking across furniture and approaching you. The physiological response can be strikingly similar: activation of the fight-or-flight system and the entire anxiety cycle associated with a phobic trigger.

Once emotional circuits are activated, the brain can respond to a vivid simulation as if it were real—and that is precisely why VR becomes such a powerful therapeutic resource.

For this reason, using VR in the treatment of phobias offers several advantages.

- The therapist has full control of the situation and can adjust intensity by modifying elements such as quantity, size, distance, or environmental conditions.
- It provides a realistic scenario without relying on imagination—something many patients find difficult.
- It allows multisensory integration, since real objects can be combined with virtual immersion—for example, gowns and gloves in the treatment of needle phobia.
- Sessions can take place entirely inside the therapeutic setting, without the need for travel.
- It is a safe, non-invasive technique that respects the patient's pace.

Even with all these benefits, what matters most is understanding that VR is not a standalone solution. It becomes stronger when integrated with other techniques and tailored to each person's individual process.

5.2 Virtual Reality and How It Can Be Amplified

In any treatment, the best outcomes come from the right combination of methods. No technology or strategy reaches its full potential on its own; its power emerges when it is woven into the broader therapeutic process. Virtual reality is no exception.

When these tools are integrated in a coordinated way, the patient tends to feel safer and respond more effectively. That is why we need to consider supports that accompany VR and AR—such as the breathing techniques we discussed in the previous chapter.

Imagine you have a needle phobia. By analyzing your profile and history, we determine what stage you are at. With that information, we can apply—within a single exposure session—at least three techniques simultaneously. Here is how that would work.

In the office, your psychologist greets you wearing a medical gown, already creating a first stimulus that evokes the hospital environment and prepares the brain for the challenge. At some point in the conversation, you put on a VR headset. In the virtual scene, you are in a medical office, about to have blood drawn. Meanwhile, through the headphones, you hear the clinician putting on gloves and other characteristic sounds of a clinical setting.

At that moment, your psychologist—now wearing real gloves—begins introducing physical sensations: they gently brush your arm with an alcohol swab exactly where, in the simulation, the blood sample will be taken.

You can smell the alcohol, see and hear the clinical environment, and feel on your skin the touch of the glove and cotton. At this point, your brain is very likely to be fully "tricked," activating the same fear reactions you experience when confronted with the real trigger.

If anxiety rises during the process, the psychologist can integrate breathing or relaxation instructions directly into the VR experience. You apply them, gradually reducing tension until you can remain exposed to the needle-related stimulus without escalating into a panic attack.

This kind of integrated intervention is not only effective in clinical practice; it is also strongly supported by recent scientific research. For example, a US study guided 23 participants to gradually approach a virtual spider. The results were striking: 83% showed a significant reduction in phobia, and some participants were able to approach a real tarantula with little to no anxiety.[3]

Of course, systematic desensitization only works when each patient's stages are respected. To reach an intense intervention like the one I just described, the person needs to be ready. In one session they may simply look at a hospital through VR. In another, they may see a nurse. In another, a syringe or a needle. Exposure must be gradual until the patient becomes sufficiently habituated to move closer to the phobic object and face it more directly.

And beyond studies and theory, clinical practice offers something equally valuable: the voices of those who take part in the process.

To illustrate this, I gathered three perspectives from people who—through their profession or organization—collaborate in systematic desensitization with my patients. I asked each of them the same question: what is it like, from your role and expertise, to participate in the treatment of phobias?

Testimonial 1

Rossana Potier, Commercial pilot
"I feel honored to be able to help people by sharing my knowledge. During therapeutic sessions, I notice that a large part of the fear of flying comes from not understanding how aviation works. Topics such as pilot training, the validity of certifications, crew preparation, airport security, aircraft maintenance, and meteorology are some of the areas we cover. Every question is clarified—and as a result, the patient

gains the confidence they need to move forward with the flight."

"The goal is to build autonomy and a sense of safety so that flying can become a pleasant experience, making my work as a pilot feel even more complete."

Testimonial 2

Professionals from Paraná Center for Hematology and Hemotherapy (HEMEPAR) – Official public health institution of the State of Paraná, Brazil

"The team involved in blood collection highlights how important it is to offer attention, care, patience, warmth, clear explanations of the procedure, and genuine appreciation for the donor—and how all of this contributes to saving lives. Supporting Nataly's patients as they work through needle and blood phobia brings us great satisfaction and motivates us to keep fulfilling our mission."

Testimonial 3

Bettina Goldenbaum, Veterinarian

"When I share my canine clients with Nataly's patients, I observe that the results are extremely positive. Dogs sense that the person with a phobia needs more time, space, and understanding—and that's how a connection begins. Unexpectedly, an almost magical interaction emerges between them. It's a rewarding experience for everyone involved!"

5.3 Biofeedback

Biofeedback is a multidisciplinary technique that, according to Schwartz (2003), uses electronic or electromechanical devices to accurately measure psychophysiological information.[4]

In simple terms, it is a method that *informs* the therapist—moment by moment—about the physiological reactions your body is experiencing. And how does that happen?

In practice, electronic devices are used to record physiological responses such as heart rate, galvanic skin response, peripheral temperature, brain activity, muscle tension, and more. These measurements reveal the person's emotional state, allowing the therapist to decide whether it is necessary to intervene, introduce a breathing technique, or continue with the procedure.

For this reason, biofeedback becomes an important tool in the treatment of phobias. If a person with a dog phobia is standing in front of a dog, the body will mirror what they feel. A common response is sweat on the fingertips—often imperceptible to the naked eye. However, with a device that measures the skin's electrical conductance, the therapist can detect the intensity of that sweating, which indicates the patient's anxiety level.

Biofeedback captures the activity of the sympathetic branch of the autonomic nervous system—the fight-or-flight response. The more stimulation the central nervous system receives, the more the sweat glands tend to activate.

In addition to these objective measures, a subjective measure can also be used by asking the patient to rate their anxiety during specific exposures. The scale ranges from one to ten, with higher numbers indicating higher anxiety. At level three, the person feels mildly anxious; at level eight, the body is already in a heightened state of alert.

This makes it far easier for the therapist to induce relaxation at the right time, because they are working with real-time data, not assumptions. It also allows the creation of a solid clinical history of progress. It is not surprising that a study by Deng and colleagues (2014) found more consistent results when patients were treated using biofeedback.[5]

Now that you understand what it is, and why it matters, it becomes much easier to grasp how VR works in practice.

1.4 In Vivo Exposure

A discussion of VR in the treatment of phobias would be incomplete without addressing in vivo exposure. After all, both virtual and real experiences are meant to be used together, alongside other therapeutic methods.

In vivo exposure, as the name suggests, involves bringing the patient closer to the feared object—always according to their stage of treatment. If someone has a cockroach phobia, you would not place a cockroach in front of them in the first session. Instead, systematic desensitization is applied through a gradual process: showing a video, using virtual reality to visualize a cockroach, working with toy insects in session, and so on.

To integrate everything you have learned so far, we will return to the cases we introduced earlier. Do you remember them? At this point, they will come to life. These women are not hypothetical cases—as you may have assumed—but real patients who faced their phobias. And now you will discover how they did it.

Case 1: Maria (Animal Phobia)

It is important to note that animal phobia covers a wide range of species—not only dogs. It can include everything from spiders to horses. In this context, Freud analyzed the case of a five-year-old boy who felt an uncontrollable fear of horses, convinced they might bite him. Known as *Little Hans,* this study illustrates how a specific phobia can emerge from environmental factors. In his case, the attention directed toward his new sister—attention he felt was denied to him—generated dissatisfaction and a sense of rejection that ultimately became displaced onto the horse, an unconscious symbol of his father.[6]

Although this case belongs to another era, the emotional logic behind it remains the same today: fear searches for an object to attach itself to. And in contemporary life, that object can take many forms. In Maria's case, it was dogs. Her fear had followed her since childhood, shaping how she related to spaces, streets, and even people. That is why working through it meant far more than "overcoming a fear": it meant reclaiming a part of her freedom.

As you follow her process—and the process of the other patients—you will notice how theory becomes lived experience, and how fear, once understood, begins to transform.

Along the way, VR became a key ally. With this tool, therapists can adjust multiple parameters: the dog's posture (sitting or standing), the distance from the avatar, the breed, whether a muzzle is used, whether another person is present beside the animal, whether the dog is leashed or loose, and the addition of barking when needed.

With this foundation, Maria's therapeutic process could be structured in a gradual and safe way. Below, you will see how

VR—combined with in vivo exposure—began to change her relationship with fear.

VR-Based Process in Maria's Sessions

1. **First approach to VR**

In the first sessions, Maria used VR goggles to practice diaphragmatic breathing and progressive muscle relaxation while watching a video of a gentle dog. Her initial anxiety level was seven.

2. **First significant drop**

In the third session, she watched the same video again, and her anxiety dropped to three. This shift marked her first window of progress.

3. **First in vivo encounter**

Before, seeing a small dog would take her to level seven; now she is at level three. For that reason, she completed her first in vivo exposure by encountering a small dog on the street.

4. **Combined exposures**

She continued alternating VR and real-life exposure— first with small dogs, then with larger dogs.

5. **Work with sound**

She watched videos of dogs barking, since that stimulus had been especially triggering for her.

6. **Expanded exposure in session**

By the tenth session, she was ready to be exposed to three dogs inside the office. She did not go into crisis.

7. **Guided interaction**

She began walking a dog on a leash, gradually increasing both the number and the size of the animals.

8. Integration into daily life

With greater confidence and emotional regulation, Maria was able to face dogs in everyday settings without triggering a phobic response.

Maria's story has an admirable ending: she is a volunteer at a non-governmental organization (NGO) that brings dogs to senior homes, special education schools, children's homes, and educational centers for animal-assisted therapy activities.

Testimonial

"The therapeutic process was a huge challenge for me. I started treatment when my fear of dogs began to affect my professional life. I work in a place where there are many dogs, and I felt unsafe just arriving. I decided to seek help, and it was the best decision I could have made. The phobia could no longer be part of me. Today, I see how much I've grown: I walk down the street with confidence, I enter places where there are dogs without anxiety, and to reinforce what I learned, I became a volunteer with an organization that offers therapeutic visits. Overcoming my phobia also transformed other areas of my life. When we face a fear, we gain the courage to face any adversity."

Case 2: Clara (Needle Phobia)

Needle and blood phobia is not only fear of a specific object—it is fear of losing control of one's own body. Unlike other phobias, where the reaction tends to be speeding up, escaping, or tensing, this phobia can trigger a particular response—the **vasovagal reflex**, which may cause dizziness, nausea, and even fainting.

From an evolutionary perspective, fainting has a protective function: by abruptly lowering heart rate and blood pressure, the body attempts to reduce blood loss in the event of a real injury. It is an ancient mechanism, designed for survival in a world where danger was physical and immediate.

But in contemporary life, that reflex can be activated by symbolic cues: a syringe seen from a distance, the smell of alcohol, a clinical laboratory, or even a scene on television. The body responds as if there were a wound—when there is not. And as with all phobias, the more the person avoids triggers, the stronger the fear becomes.

In Clara's case, that mechanism kept her from having blood tests for four years. It was not "just fear"—it was the feeling that her own body betrayed her in medical environments. That is why virtual reality can be so valuable in this type of phobia: it allows the triggering stimuli to be recreated step by step, without the person losing control. Settings such as hospitals, dental offices, or laboratories can be carefully graded—adjusting distance, intensity, sounds, instruments, and context.

VR-Based Process in Clara's Sessions

1. First contact with VR

Clara had gone four years without a blood test. For that reason, the first VR sessions were carefully adapted to her anxiety level.

2. Becoming familiar with the syringe

In the third session, she was exposed to a real syringe and learned to handle it without triggering extreme reactions.

3. **Progressive desensitization**

To move forward, another person was invited into the session for a superficial finger prick. At the start of the session Clara's anxiety level was ten and by the end of the session it two.

4. **Strengths as an anchor**

She completed the strengths-identification exercise described in Chapter 4, section 4.2.3 Uncover Meaning and the Joy of Being Alive, which reinforced her sense of capability and agency.

5. **Hypnosis and emotional regulation**

Hypnosis techniques accompanied the entire systematic desensitization process until, when observing a real blood draw, anxiety no longer emerged.

Today, Clara is a blood donor.

Testimonial

"Knowing there was someone who understood my pain and was willing to help me was essential. I achieved what I believed was impossible: I made my first blood donation. Today I say with pride that I belong to the first generation in my family to overcome a phobia. I get blood tests, I go into hospitals, and I get vaccinated. I recovered quality of life—and above all, I recovered the ability to know how I am. Everything became possible thanks to this therapeutic process."

Case 3: Talita (Fear of Flying)

Talita came to therapy after years of avoiding any form of air travel. She was not afraid of heights, but of something more intimate: losing control of her own body. She would vomit before boarding, sweat at the thought of takeoff, and often cancel the trip just hours before departure.

As surprising as it may sound, fear of flying is not born in the sky—it is born on the ground, in personal histories shaped by loss of control, vulnerability, or catastrophic anticipation. It is estimated that around 10% of the population experiences fear of flying so intensely that they reorganize their lives to avoid the sky.[7] But what is most striking—and rarely said out loud—is that the airplane is not always the true problem. Often, the trigger is the body itself, when it interprets the flight as an inescapable space.

Cantón-Dutari's research (1974) suggested that—even without seeing an airplane—the mere sound of an engine or the auditory simulation of a cabin could activate the fear circuit.[8] What does that mean? That fear of flying is not fear of the air, but fear of the *internal scenario* we project onto it.

From a psychobiological perspective, the airplane is not just a machine—it becomes a symbol. At an unconscious level, flying activates three essential conflicts: the sensation of losing control ("My life is not in my hands"), separation from safe territory ("I am far from what sustains me"), and catastrophic anticipation ("Something could happen, and I will not be able to prevent it").

Today, VR allows us to enter that inner landscape with remarkable precision: from the road to the airport to the sound of the plane doors closing; from the takeoff lights to the subtle, moment-to-moment movement of turbulence.

Everything can be adjusted: weather, seat, distance to the wing, number of passengers, even the tone of voice of the cabin crew.

VR-Based Process in Talita's Sessions

1. Psychoeducation with a commercial pilot

Talita learned that turbulence is not danger; that an airplane is not "held up" in the air but moves through it; and that pilots train for more hours than a passenger will fly in an entire lifetime. Information does not erase fear—but it removes the mystery that feeds it.

2. First flights in virtual reality

In a simulation of a calm flight, her initial anxiety was surprisingly low. This allowed us to gradually add elements that had previously paralyzed her: rain, vibrations, and cabin announcements.

3. Integrated regulation techniques

Each increase in difficulty was paired with diaphragmatic breathing, bodily grounding, and progressive muscle relaxation. Virtual reality allowed us to move forward with no real-world risk—but with the full emotional intensity of a "real flight."

4. In vivo exposure

Talita entered a real airplane, accompanied. She did not fly—she simply sat down. Then she repeated this process. Eventually, one day, she took off.

Talita did not only manage to fly without panic. She achieved something even more important—she redefined her relationship with her own body. She no longer interprets her sensations as danger signals, but as normal fluctuations of a sensitive nervous system.

Today she enjoys reading or playing on her phone while flying. And each time she takes off, she remembers: that sky she once feared now belongs to her, too.

Testimonial

"Treatment with virtual reality was a turning point in my life. The phobia locked me in; therapy gave me the key back. Today I am free to see the world—and to live the life I once only imagined."

Case 4: Jéssica (Closed Spaces and Agoraphobia)

We often associate claustrophobia with movie scenes—characters trapped in tunnels or tiny rooms—but claustrophobia is not born in outer spaces. It is born in inner spaces: in the feeling that the body itself is a place you cannot escape.

This reaction can occur even in everyday situations where there is no immediate objective danger, such as an elevator or a movie theater. For the human mind, the thought "I can't get out" is enough to trigger the alarm system.

A similar mechanism occurs in agoraphobia, which does not depend on the shape of the place, but on the emotional experience it produces. Someone may feel panic in a crowded shopping mall—but also in a wide-open area. The trigger is not the environment, but the internal interpretation: "If something happens to me here, I won't be able to leave, I won't be able to ask for help, I won't be able to hold myself together."

That is why many cases involve a combination of

anticipatory fear and avoidance. Some studies, such as Chambless and colleagues (1982), have pointed to an association between agoraphobia, higher social anxiety, and difficulties with assertiveness.[9]

From a deeper lens, both phobias share an essential conflict: fear of losing autonomy in spaces where the body believes it could become trapped—physically or emotionally.

It is an ancient, biological fear that echoes experiences of confinement, blockage, immobilization, or helplessness. In these cases, the physical space merely activates an emotional space that already exists.

For Jéssica, just thinking about using an elevator or boarding an airplane—places where she could not control the exit—was terrifying. Her body reacted before she could think rationally: sweating, shaking, feeling suffocated. Still, she chose to face it.

VR-Based Process in Jéssica's Sessions

1. Early sessions

Jéssica shared something that shaped the direction of treatment: for years she had traveled only by car, and only after taking medication that put her to sleep. A previous experience—being stuck inside a vehicle for hours—had left her body with the impression that small spaces were not safe.

2. First safe contact with fear

To begin, we practiced diaphragmatic breathing and progressive muscle relaxation while Jéssica used VR. The simulation recreated a small, quiet elevator with no abrupt movement. We were not trying to "overcome" her fear—we were teaching her body that it could stay in the environment without escaping.

3. When the body began to remember

In the fourth session, we continued with VR scenarios calibrated to her anxiety level. Each time the simulation activated her internal alarm, we returned to breathing, grounding, and reconnecting with the present reality. It was delicate work: teaching her body that it could feel fear without interpreting it as real confinement.

4. First challenge in the real world

When her anxiety in the virtual elevator dropped to level four, we moved to the first in vivo exposure: going up two floors in the elevator of her own building. Her hands trembled, her breathing sped up—and she stayed. It was a turning point: her body proved to itself that it could pass through the experience without being overwhelmed.

5. Reclaiming autonomy, step by step

Over time, Jéssica was able to enter elevators alone, even those tighter than the ones she had faced at the beginning. In parallel, we began VR sessions simulating an airplane: long aisles, doors closing, crowded cabins. Each exposure built a new layer of autonomy, dismantling the belief that "escaping" was the only option.

Today, Jéssica feels safe in enclosed spaces—not because fear vanished magically, but because she learned not to interpret it as a sentence, but as a passing sensation her body can hold.

Testimonial

"I decided to seek help when I realized how much I was losing by letting fear run my life. When I discovered the virtual reality method, I regained hope. Each session was a small victory—first with the headset, then in real life. The first time I entered an elevator alone after years, I felt something in me return. There were days I wanted to give up, but I learned that facing fear is also building courage. Today I no longer see the elevator or the airplane as enemies—we coexist peacefully. Having overcome my phobia is indescribable. Now I know I am much bigger than any fear."

These stories show—powerfully—the strength of integrated treatment in phobia recovery. Each person walked a different path, yet all moved forward thanks to a precise combination of therapeutic techniques: from in vivo exposure to the specialized use of virtual reality. No method replaces another; they complement each other, amplify each other, and create a safe ground where body and mind can learn to respond differently.

And to sustain that process, we work with a compass: the COURAGE acrostic described in Chapter 4. This therapeutic sequence guides each step—when fear rises, we return to the body, steady the breath, regain focus, adjust the dose of exposure, and above all restore choice. The goal is not "to feel no fear," but to move through fear without abandoning yourself.

And perhaps the most transformative truth is this: a phobia can be overcome. Every one of these people arrived in treatment believing they had already tried everything. What they discovered was that there were more pathways than they could imagine. With the right approach, professional support, and a process that respects one's pace, freedom becomes possible. If you also live with fear at this level, do not doubt that you can move forward. Each person's timeline is different—but the movement is real. As Maria said at the end of her process: "I stopped feeling phobic. That isn't just clinical improvement—it is a new way of inhabiting life."

6.
PHOBIAS AND THEIR MANIFESTATIOS TODAY

From the outside, Felipe lived a life that anyone else would consider "doing well." He had just been promoted. His company celebrated him publicly. His family repeated, with genuine excitement, how proud they were. On social media, the comments stacked up like an optimistic chorus: "You deserve it," "You've always been so dedicated," "You inspire me!"

He responded the way someone is expected to respond when they are "fine": he thanked people, cracked jokes, chose the right emojis, even posted a funny GIF. To any casual observer, his profile radiated fulfillment.

Behind the screen, however, there was another scene. To capture the photo he posted, he repeated the same smile over and over, trying to keep his face from revealing the exhaustion he carried inside. Only one image managed to sustain the fiction.

Anyone who saw that photo would imagine a night of toasts and celebration. But the moment he posted it, Felipe turned off his phone and returned to the silence of his living room. For months, his life had been shrinking: home, computer, bed. Each week he went out less, spoke less, moved less.

It was not work that confined him. It was fear. His body had begun to feel like unstable territory, difficult to inhabit in front of other people.

His brother Luciano had been trying for more than two months to get him out of the house: a quick dinner, a family barbecue, a visit to the bar Luciano had recently opened. The answer was always the same: "Another day." And that "another day" never came.

Because Felipe continued completing tasks, replying to messages, and maintaining the appearance of normality, no one suspected something deeper was happening. Not his brother. Not his family. Not his virtual friends. They saw functioning; he was surviving.

Today, this pattern is becoming increasingly common because avoidance is easy to disguise. You can "be there" without truly being there. Meetings happen on a screen. Relationships unfold through messages. Recognition comes through metrics. In the short time, the body feels relief. But it also learns a dangerous association: **avoidance equals safety**.

The last time he went out was out of necessity: the pantry was empty. He walked to the corner store with his body rigid, bought the essentials, and hurried back as if the outside air itself might break him. He closed the door of his home office and felt a strange kind of relief—not the relief of coming home, but the relief of someone who has escaped.

At first, working from home had felt like a privilege: quiet, autonomy, time. But over the months, that quiet began to hollow out. And eventually a hollow space becomes an abyss. What started as comfort turned into isolation. What began as preference became avoidance.

There were days he did not even get out of bed. He called it rest. His body knew it was retreat. The next day, sitting in front of the computer, he tried to gather what had scattered inside him. He worked in a state of inertia, with a fragmented mind, as if each task pulled him farther away from himself.

This pattern had not appeared out of nowhere. Felipe had always been like this—though as a child, no one knew how to read it correctly. His withdrawal was interpreted as shyness. His fear of making mistakes was labeled sensitivity. His discomfort in groups became "a quiet personality." His silence was praised as good manners.

Being watched made him tense. The mere possibility of failing could flood him with dread. Expectations pressed in from every side—first coming from others, then becoming his own—and left him restless. Without a single conscious decision, his body built a defense: tightening, reading threat into ordinary moments, and hiding what he felt.

What no one recognized then was that his history contained many of the elements that, over time, often shape social phobia: self-worth tied to performance, a silent emotional demand to "be good," and extreme sensitivity to judgment. Early on, Felipe learned that being seen carried risk, that taking up space required caution, and that vulnerability needed to be carefully managed.

In many family systems, staying quiet, adapting, and not causing discomfort becomes the safest way to maintain belonging. Felipe absorbed that logic without words. And when his body began to change—during the stage when identity, desire, and shame search for a place—he understood that his presence could be observed, evaluated, even deemed "too much."

Felipe's symptoms did not appear as a rupture, but as refuge: a silent way to protect himself from exposure, even at the cost of emotional freedom.

Felipe's story is fictional, but it is deeply rooted in clinical reality. It reflects an increasingly common scenario: individuals who develop social phobia and, over time, move into depressive processes. What begins as protection gradually becomes isolation.

And when a person stops circulating through the world—stops feeling seen, heard, needed—they do not only lose confidence. They lose meaning. That is where sadness stops being temporary and becomes a state.

Clinical research reinforces this connection. A classic study by Versiani and colleagues (1994), involving 250 individuals with social phobia, found that 29.6% presented comorbidity with major depression and 18.4% developed dysthymia (chronic depression).[1] Similar findings appear in later research. In a study with 63 patients, D'El Rey and Freedner (2006) observed that in 62 cases, the first depressive episode emerged after the onset of social phobia, and only in one case did both conditions appear simultaneously.[2] These findings confirm what clinical practice reveals daily: when fear of exposure becomes a way of living, emotional isolation opens the door to depression.

Comorbidity, however, is not limited to the relationship between social phobia and depression. In mental health, comorbidity refers to the coexistence of two or more disorders within the same individual—conditions that often interact and reinforce one another. From this perspective, the same mechanism—one condition preparing the ground for another—appears across multiple clinically relevant combinations. Alongside attention-deficit/hyperactivity disorder (ADHD), social phobia frequently coexists with other anxiety disorders, such as generalized anxiety disorder and panic disorder, as well as substance use and avoidant personality traits. These combinations create clinical pictures that cannot be understood—or treated—in fragments.[4]

During the school years, children with ADHD—a neurodevelopmental condition affecting self-regulation—often face repeated misunderstanding from adults and peers. This is not a lack of effort. Their brains struggle more with sustaining attention, inhibiting impulses, and organizing behavior, even when motivation is present. They receive frequent criticism for being "distracted" or "not trying hard enough," and experience moments of public shame that leave lasting marks on self-esteem. Without anyone explicitly naming it, the message repeats: something about me does not fit.

Over time, as experiences of error and exposure accumulate, fear stops being linked to a single situation and begins to generalize. It is no longer just about being distracted in class or making a mistake on an assignment. It becomes the constant anticipation of failing again. To protect themselves, the person learns to avoid: they avoid speaking, avoid trying, avoid showing up. Fear becomes a silent organizer of behavior.

Different phobic manifestations unfold along this same continuum. In some cases, fear presents as social phobia. In others, it appears as a persistent fear of making mistakes, disappointing others, or losing control in front of an audience. Even patterns like nomophobia can be understood through this lens: beyond technological dependence, the device becomes a refuge, buffering exposure and temporarily easing the anxiety of being fully seen.

Understanding phobias from this perspective is not about reducing them to diagnostic labels or exaggerated reactions to the world. It is about recognizing that, in many cases, fear was a solution before it became a challenge: a way to preserve belonging, avoid shame, or protect emotional integrity when no other resources were available.

From this view, suffering stops being an "error" that must be eliminated and can begin to be understood as an experience that—however painful—carries meaning. Not because pain is desirable, but because even in the middle of it, a person still retains the capacity to take a position, choose an attitude, and rebuild significance.

And yet, what once functioned as refuge can, over time, become a silent prison. That is why therapeutic work is not about eliminating fear, but about elaborating it: understanding its origin, listening to what it is trying to protect, and opening space for new responses.

In the next chapter, we will explore how to begin that process—and what happens when fear stops governing life and becomes a signal that can be understood, integrated, and transformed.

7.
TRANSFORMING YOUR RELATIONSHIP WITH FEAR

Before it became a symptom, fear was a solution.

Fear emerged as an adaptive response to an experience that overwhelmed the resources available at that time. Its purpose was not to create suffering, but to protect what felt essential: connection, belonging, and integrity. When there were no words, no options, and not enough support, fear offered a way to stay safe.

That is why transforming your relationship with fear does not mean eliminating it—or confronting it as if it were an enemy. It means understanding what need it was trying to meet, and in what context it was learned, recognizing that what once protected you can, over time, become a limitation.

In childhood, fear is rarely processed through words or reasoning: it is learned and absorbed. A child does not yet have emotional distance, symbolic resources, or autonomy to metabolize what is happening. When an experience threatens safety, love, or belonging, the organism responds by organizing protective strategies. Silence can become a way to maintain the bond. Avoidance can become a way to reduce exposure. Tension can become an attempt to hold yourself together when something feels too much. These are not conscious decisions—they are silent learnings that, over time, can solidify into patterns.

With time, these protective strategies do not remain only in the body: they also organize into beliefs that shape how we think, decide, and relate.

We can recognize these strategies in many of the beliefs that quietly run adult life—often without full awareness. They do not always appear as explicit thoughts, but as silent inner commands: "You can't trust," "I have to handle everything," "I'm not capable." At their origin, these beliefs served a defensive function. They helped sustain adaptation in a context where there were no other viable alternatives.

Conflict arises when these commands keep operating automatically even when conditions have changed. What once protected begins to restrict. A person does not avoid because they cannot do something, but because—often unconsciously—they remain loyal to internal rules that once created meaning and safety in early stages of life.

7.1 Anger as a Silenced Root

Beliefs are not the only force that sustains fear. There is a deeper emotion—often more forbidden in childhood—beneath many phobic structures: **anger**.

From a very early age, many children learn that expressing anger toward parents or caregivers is dangerous. It can threaten love, belonging, protection—or even survival. And so that anger is not expressed: it is suppressed. But postponed emotions do not disappear; they reorganize.

When anger cannot be consciously felt or directed toward its true origin, it seeks a safer destination. What cannot be felt becomes fear. What cannot be confronted becomes avoidance. And what cannot be named moves into the body as symptom. In this movement, fear functions like a disguise: a socially acceptable expression of an emotion that, at the time, had no permission to exist.

From a psychodynamic perspective, a phobia is not explained solely by fear itself, but by the conflict that sustains it. It is the result of unresolved tensions between dependence and autonomy, loyalty and individuation, attachment and separation. The symptom freezes that conflict in time—offering protection, while also keeping the person imprisoned within the same dynamics.[1]

Paradoxically, the anger that was once silenced can become the key to liberation. When it is recognized and integrated, it stops being destructive and becomes movement. It carries the energy needed to break invisible bonds, dissolve emotional dependencies, and question patterns of submission that often extend into adult life—emotionally and financially.

Many people remain trapped not because they lack courage or intelligence, but because their anger never became conscious. Without access to this vital energy, they remain loyal to old dynamics, repeating them through fear instead of transforming them through self-affirmation.

Transforming your relationship with fear, therefore, does not mean eliminating anger—it means recovering it. Giving it a place, a meaning, and a direction. When anger is recognized instead of denied, fear no longer needs to speak on its behalf. And what once manifested as a phobic prison can begin to transform into a bridge toward autonomy, responsibility, and inner freedom.

When these conflicts remain unresolved, they rarely stay confined to the inner world; they tend to organize themselves within relational and family systems as well. From this perspective, it is worth looking at the invisible dynamics that often shape bonds—just as the systemic approach describes them.

One of the most well-known references in this perspective is Bert Hellinger, who described how certain invisible dynamics can organize suffering and relationships within a family system.[2] Drawing on his own life trajectory, he emphasized the importance of listening to internal signals before acting. In contexts of absolute uncertainty, he discovered that orientation does not always come from the outside, but from an inner perception that integrates sensation, intuition, and reality.

Imagine the following scenario: you are a soldier during World War II. You have been captured and are a prisoner. In an attempt to survive, you hide inside a train car. At each stop, you must decide whether it is time to get out or remain—without being able to look outside, without knowing where the train is headed. What if the next destination is another prison camp?

Hellinger lived this experience. And it was in that waiting—suspended between fear and possibility—that he understood something fundamental: the need to listen inwardly. With no external certainty, he learned to register internal signals and connect them to the few available clues—sounds, limited sight, bodily sensations—that could offer even minimal reference for safety. From that dialogue between inner and outer, an intuition emerged that told him when it was the right moment to leave the train car.

During that extreme experience, fear was not an enemy to defeat, but a signal to listen to. It was not about reacting impulsively, but about staying attentive, available, connected to what was happening inside and outside. Survival did not depend on controlling the environment—impossible in that context—but on developing an inner presence capable of discerning the right moment to act. That learning was not theoretical: it was embodied, intuitive, profoundly human.

That is why integrating fear is an act of connection: recognizing the internal roots of a reaction and, at the same time, the external factors that shaped it. When fear stops being interpreted as an obstacle and begins to be understood as a signal, it becomes possible to read it, integrate it, and transform it. From that understanding, the way Hellinger described the invisible dynamics that organize human systems begins to make sense.

Hellinger observed that in every system—especially the family system—there are principles that, when disrupted, generate deep tensions that may express themselves as emotional symptoms, persistent fears, or relational blockages. He referred to these principles as **systemic laws**.

1. The Law of Order (or Hierarchy)

The law of order states that those who arrived earlier in a system take precedence over those who came later. In the family context, this means recognizing and respecting the place of the parents as the origin of life. When this order is disrupted—for example, when a child takes on emotional responsibilities or roles that do not belong to them—heavy inner burdens often arise, which may manifest as anxiety, guilt, or persistent fear.

2. The Law of Belonging

The law of belonging refers to a fundamental human need: every member of a system has the right to belong. Exclusion—whether explicit or silent—creates compensatory movements. In many cases, intense fears, insecurity, or social avoidance can be understood as unconscious attempts to not lose a bond, or to secure a place within the system where the person longs to belong.

3. The Law of Balance

The law of balance refers to the need for reciprocity in relationships. In adult relationships, giving and receiving must remain in relatively balanced proportion for the bond to be healthy. The only relationship that structurally allows imbalance is the parent-child relationship: children receive life, and later, they "return" that movement by giving life to others.[3]

From this perspective, fear does not appear in isolation or by chance. Often, it signals an unresolved systemic tension.

For example, a person who avoids public speaking or feels deeply insecure in social situations may be expressing—at a symptomatic level—a difficulty connected to belonging: an unconscious fear of not having a place, of being rejected, or of not being recognized within the system they are trying to join.

Perhaps during childhood—or at a significant moment in life—the person felt they did not belong to their family system, even without consciously remembering it. This may have occurred through a misunderstanding—such as believing parents paid more attention to a younger sibling and therefore loved them more, through a distortion—feeling different from the family and concluding one is in the wrong place, or even through a phrase that was heard and interpreted in a way that installed the experience of non-belonging.

The result? An insecure adult who struggles to feel part of other systems—professional, social, or emotional—and who may become more vulnerable to relational difficulties, including social phobia.

This is only one example, but it illustrates why these laws matter when exploring whether they might lie at the roots of your fears. It is worth pausing and looking inward with honesty.

1. **Do I feel I occupy a place that is not mine?** Do I behave as if I must take care of my parents or assume responsibilities that are not mine?

2. **Do I feel I belong in my family?** Deep down, do I feel I am in the right place when I am with my relatives?

3. **Is there balance between what I give and what I receive?** In my relationships, can I feel genuine reciprocity?

These are simple questions, but profoundly revealing—not to judge you, but to understand you. As these dynamics become more conscious, fear loses rigidity and becomes more legible. And when fear can be read, it can also be reframed.

For that, the process requires something essential: **inner availability**. This means relaxing, suspending judgment, and allowing answers to emerge without forcing them, not from demand, but from listening. Only in that state is it possible to perceive what is truly operating beneath fear.

When this availability is absent, negative thoughts tend to occupy the entire psychic space. They distort reality—and if they are not recognized early, they multiply quickly, organizing inner life around threat.

Imagine the following scene. The day is pleasant; sunlight spills over the grass, and everything seems ideal for rest. You are with a friend, laughing at jokes you do not find funny—just to avoid feeling awkward. It is Sunday. You chose the place carefully. You prepared everything. In front of you, there is a chocolate cake. Just looking at it awakens desire.

In that same space, an ant approaches. You see it and brush it away easily. The cake remains safe. But soon, many more appear. The first one was not alone—it brought reinforcements. And what seemed insignificant begins to overwhelm you.

That is how negative thoughts work. On their own, they can seem harmless—almost irrelevant. But when they chain together, when they are not observed or contained, they can invade the inner scene and take control. Not because they are powerful in themselves, but because they operate without being questioned.

That is why working with fear is not about fighting thoughts or trying to eliminate them by force. It is about recognizing the loop, interrupting the automatic replay, and reclaiming an inner stance from which you can choose how to relate to your inner experience. When the mind stops reacting with inertia, fear loses strength and begins to transform.

This process requires a prior step: learning to observe thoughts without becoming trapped in them. In earlier chapters, we explored a simple and effective way to do this through the COURAGE technique, which can be summarized in three essential movements.

1. Pause.
2. Bring the thought back to rational ground.
3. Move the mind to an inner place of safety.

However, this work goes beyond understanding and regulating negative thoughts. It also involves **replacing** them—offering new images and meanings to the inner world. Here, the contributions of Milton Erickson become especially valuable.[4]

Erickson, a foundational figure in modern hypnotic approaches, understood that the unconscious does not respond primarily to logical arguments, but to images, symbols, and metaphors. From childhood, we are deeply responsive to stories: a single image can have far greater impact than a rational explanation.

To say someone has a "heart of stone" immediately evokes a concrete image—solid, impenetrable. That image communicates far more than the abstract statement that the person struggles with emotional bonding.

The same happens when we use metaphors to reinterpret internal beliefs. Their effect is often deeper and more durable than a purely rational restructuring.

Consider, for example, someone who repeatedly heard criticisms about their appearance in childhood and eventually absorbed the inner command: "I'm not beautiful—I'm ugly." This belief affects self-esteem, weakens confidence, and can foster anxiety. A metaphor can open a different path.

The story of *The Ugly Duckling* illustrates this clearly. In the tale, the problem was not in the duckling, but in the limited gaze of those who could not recognize who it was—or what it could become. What was rejected was, in truth, the expression of its singularity.

Beyond its apparent simplicity, the story reveals something essential: many negative inner commands do not describe personal truth, but other people's interpretations—absorbed without being questioned.

When someone grows up hearing repeated criticism—about appearance, worth, or capacity—they may build a self-image shaped by insecurity. And over time, insecurity often becomes dependence: a constant need for external support in order to feel safe.

Dependence offers momentary safety, but it comes with a cost. In adult bonds, when one person leans too heavily on another to stay upright, balance breaks. From the perspective of the law of balance, giving and receiving lose proportion, and the relationship begins to organize itself around inequality.

So how do you change your relationship with the fear of insecurity?

Imagine a bird that has just landed on a tree branch. The tree is strong and sturdy—yet wind shakes its branches. The bird's body also moves with that sway.

Should it be afraid? Does it need to search for another branch—more rigid, more stable—in order to feel safe?

No. The bird does not place its trust in the branch, but in its wings. It knows that if the branch breaks, it can fly. Its safety does not depend on external support, but on its own capacity to hold itself in the air.

The same happens when a person recognizes their inner power. Safety stops living outside, dependence loosens its grip, and fear begins to transform—not because it disappears, but because it no longer governs decisions.

This is the foundation of every deep process of integration: shifting the axis of safety from the external to the internal. When a person stops seeking support exclusively outside themselves, a more mature reorganization of identity becomes possible.

In many cases, for this inner movement to sustain itself over time, something else becomes necessary: **meaning**. Viktor E. Frankl developed this understanding from his own experience of extreme suffering. In *Man's Search for Meaning*, he proposed that human beings can find meaning in life in three ways.[5]

1.   By experiencing something valuable or encountering another person authentically.
2.   By creating or offering something through one's actions.
3.   By adopting a conscious attitude toward unavoidable suffering.

This third point may be the most challenging. It does not mean denying pain or justifying it, but recognizing that even in circumstances that cannot be changed, a person still retains the capacity to choose how to position themselves in relation to what they live.

From this perspective, elaborating fear is not eliminating it or "overcoming" it as if it were an external obstacle. It is understanding the place it occupied, the function it served, and the moment it ceased to be necessary. It is recognizing that what once protected can also transform when it no longer matches the present reality.

Along this path, we have seen how fear organizes itself in the body, solidifies into beliefs, intertwines with unexpressed emotions, inscribes itself into relationships, and finds form within the systems we belong to. We have also seen that transformation does not happen by force, but through understanding, presence, and meaning.

When fear can be read—rather than battled—it stops governing life. It becomes a signal, not a limit. And from that place a person can begin to choose to sustain themselves from within, reorganize their bonds and orienting their experience toward something worth living.

To give new meaning to fear is, ultimately, an act of psychological maturity: moving from survival to inhabiting one's own life with awareness, responsibility, and direction.

8.
SPIRITUALITY AND INNER SUPPORT

There comes a moment in a phobia when the mind no longer convinces and the body no longer obeys. The heart races, the breath shortens, reality narrows. And the person does not need more explanations—they need support. Not an external support that promises to control everything, but an inner anchor that brings them back to center when fear feels bigger than willpower.

That is what I mean when I speak of spirituality. Not religion, but an intimate dimension that can help you move through fear without being defined by it. In phobia, the world shrinks. Spirituality—understood as a connection to something wider than the symptom—can restore spaciousness: meaning, belonging, trust, direction.

Whatever you believe, it is important to recognize that your beliefs have value.

The influence of spirituality on health processes has been observed even in medicine. Some medical schools have incorporated this dimension into their training, after recognizing that healing processes are often deeply linked to spirituality.[1] Likewise, various healthcare institutions and research lines have highlighted the importance of considering a patient's spiritual dimension—when it is meaningful for them—as part of truly person-centered care.[2]

These acknowledgments are not related to any specific faith. They point to something more essential: the understanding that human beings do not face fear only with mental or physical resources.

When a phobia breaks in, it is not just thought that gets overwhelmed—it is the feeling of being alone in front of something that seems uncontrollable. And it is precisely here that spirituality can become an ally.

Faith—understood here not as dogma, but as connection—offers what fear tries to steal: **trust**. Trust that not everything depends on control; that there is a support larger than the symptom; that human experience is not limited to the immediate threat.

When a person believes—in something, in someone, or in a force that transcends them—an inner sense of shelter is activated. Even if it cannot be seen, it can be felt. And when it is felt, the body stops living in a constant state of alarm.

Clinically, we know that the felt sense of safety is one of the most important factors for deactivating fight, flight, or freeze. In this sense, faith does not erase fear—but it introduces an inner ground from which fear no longer needs to occupy the entire psychic space.

Belief does not mean denying reality or waiting for magic solutions. It means accepting that not everything can be controlled—and still choosing to trust.

Trust introduces an experience fear tries to cancel: the ability to wait without collapsing. When a person learns to wait—not from resignation, but from presence—anxiety decreases. And when anxiety decreases, fear loses intensity.

Faith also opens space for another essential experience: love. Not an idealized or romantic love, but a love that does not demand constant proof of worthiness. Where fear installs guilt, love introduces acceptance. And without guilt, the inner system can finally loosen its grip.

From approaches such as psychogenealogy and transgenerational work, some authors have described that certain phobias and intense anxieties are not always fully understood through personal biography only. In some cases, they may be linked to emotional memories of family: unresolved grief, abrupt losses, silenced violence, stories organized around fear. The body can react as if it "remembers" what could not be spoken—not as conscious memory, but as emotional imprint and automatic response.

Mark Wolynn describes, for example, the case of a woman who had an intense, inexplicable fear of water, accompanied by severe physical symptoms, despite never having lived any personal traumatic experience related to drowning. The symptom only began to make sense when it was revealed that her grandmother had lost a brother to drowning in childhood—something never spoken of in the family. The fear did not belong to the patient's conscious biography, but to the family system's emotional memory, transmitted through silence, unprocessed anguish, and hypervigilance.[3]

Anne Ancelin Schützenberger reports similar situations in patients with recurrent panic attacks that arose without apparent cause. In several of these cases, the symptom coincided with ages, dates, or contexts linked to early deaths, hidden abortions, or traumatic losses experienced by previous generations. When those family griefs could be named and acknowledged, the intensity of the panic decreased significantly—as though the body no longer needed to remember what had never been symbolized.[4]

In such cases, the symptom can be understood as an unconscious loyalty: fear keeps alive a story that never found language. Not to punish, but to belong. And when one tries to "eliminate" fear without listening to it, resistance can appear—not because the person wants to suffer, but because the symptom has become associated with the bond that helped them endure.

In some relationships, fear serves a silent function: it organizes closeness, legitimizes overprotection, sustains dependency, and preserves roles of control. Not out of malice, but out of emotional need. When one person is afraid, another may feel necessary. When one person does not move forward, another maintains their role.

This is where an ethical and spiritual point becomes fundamental: **caring is not controlling**. Accompanying is not preventing someone else's movement. Protecting does not mean keeping the other small so you can feel safe.

When someone else's fear becomes a way to regulate one's own emotions, a deep block forms. Not only does fear become fixed—so does the possibility of growth. Recognizing these dynamics is not about assigning blame; it is about returning awareness, freedom, and movement to where fear has stopped life.

Because just as a phobia requires inner support, it also needs an environment that does not feed on fear—an environment that does not reinforce it to soothe its own insecurities, and that knows how to distinguish care from control. Learning to care, in this context, is also learning to let go.

And this opens a practical question: **how do we accompany someone without reinforcing fear?**

Accompanying a person with a phobia takes more than good intentions. It requires lucidity about your own fears, your own limits, and—above all—about a silent temptation: keeping the other fragile so you do not have to face your own insecurity.

Many times, without realizing it, we confuse care with control. Protection with immobility. Presence with overprotection.

Accompanying is not preventing the other from feeling fear. It is tolerating your own discomfort while the other learns to hold themselves.

Because when someone we love has a phobia, fear does not live only in the one who suffers from it.

It also settles in those around them: in the urgency to calm, in the need to fix, in the impulse to anticipate so nothing "goes wrong."

But fear does not dissolve when someone walks for another. It transforms when someone walks beside them.

8.1 Do Not Feed the Fear—Hold the Presence

Fear expands when it becomes the absolute center of the scene. Every time someone avoids for the other, justifies for the other, or explains for the other, the implicit message is the same: "You can't." And that message—however loving—weakens.

Many phobias are not maintained only by the original fear, but by the network of care built around it. The more the environment adapts to fear, the more reasons fear has to remain. Not out of malice, but out of coherence: the system learns that fear "works."

Supporting is not removing obstacles from the path—and it is not pushing. It is staying present without taking the other person's place. When someone stays beside you, fear begins to lose centrality.

Clinically, we know that constant attention placed on fear amplifies it. The body reads hypervigilance as confirmation of danger. In contrast, a calm presence—non-invasive, non-anxious—helps the nervous system regulate. Not because anything is explained, but because the body learns through resonance.

In a crisis, you do not need to convince, debate the logic of fear, or validate the threat. What helps most is anchoring the experience in the concrete and the present: the body, the surroundings, the breath, reality still existing beyond the symptom.

Gently guiding the person to notice what is around them—people nearby, sounds, movement—can help the nervous system register something essential: not everything is **immediate danger**. Sometimes, a simple, structured task—counting by twos, naming visible objects, even briefly switching languages—can redirect attention from panic circuits to more organized cognitive activity and reduce arousal.

Shifting focus does not deny what the person feels. It prevents fear from taking over everything. Because when fear becomes total, there is no room left for resource, experience, or trust.

Calm is not transmitted by words.
It is transmitted by inner state.

And here is an uncomfortable but necessary truth: supporting someone with a phobia requires the supporter to tolerate their own anxiety:

- tolerating **not** intervening
- tolerating **not** controlling
- tolerating **not** being indispensable.

Sometimes the most caring gesture is not doing more. It is doing less—and being more.

8.2 Turn the Gaze Toward What Is Gained—Not Toward Fear

This is not about denying fear or forcing positive thinking. Nor is it about demanding bravery too soon. Support is more subtle: it helps fear stop being the only criterion organizing life.

With a phobia, much psychic energy gets captured by avoidance and by anticipating what could go wrong. The horizon narrows. And gradually, fear begins to decide not only what is avoided, but also which relationships cool, which movements are postponed, and which experiences remain suspended.

So instead of saying "don't be afraid," a question that truly encourages change, when asked without pressure, is: **"What parts of your life have been on pause since fear started deciding for you?"**

Not to force an answer, but to allow what fear has eclipsed to re-emerge: desires, connections, possibilities.

I remember a patient with a phobia of cats. He avoided any conversation about them and, without noticing, also avoided an important professional bond: his boss, who loved talking about her cats. In session, we did not push confrontation; we explored something simple. When he imagined being able to speak naturally about something meaningful to her, a different motivation appeared. Fear was no longer pushing him—connection was pulling him.

This reveals something essential: **when the focus shifts from danger to meaning, fear begins to lose its organizing power.**

8.3 Movement As an Ally

Physical activity can be a powerful ally in managing fear and anxiety—provided it is chosen, not imposed. The goal is not "exercise as obligation," but movement that feels pleasurable and respectful of the person's emotional moment.

When the body moves in a way that generates enjoyment, the nervous system tends to settle; the body feels more capable, less trapped, more alive. In states of anticipatory anxiety, that effect can be deeply regulating.

It can help to anticipate, by inviting movement weeks

before a trigger situation (for example, a medical exam, a social event) so the body arrives less loaded. Another option is creating a shared habit. When both people enjoy it, movement stops being "a technique" and becomes a space of bond, consistency, and care.

8.4 Supporting is Not Reinforcing Fear

Support is not only about what happens when fear spikes. It is also about how the relationship is structured over time. Here a common confusion appears: emotional support is not the same as reinforcing fear.

Reinforcing fear means organizing the bond around the symptom—avoiding for the person, constantly adapting life around what might overwhelm them. Supporting means staying available without replacing them—offering closeness without taking their place.

I remember a teenager with a fear of flying. Her parents were loving and attentive—yet the fear had become a central reference point in the family bond. In a session, the mother shared: "I took a flight with turbulence and couldn't stop thinking about my daughter. I kept imagining how awful it would have been for her."

There was no bad intention—only love. But repeated often, this kind of association quietly communicates: the fear is the lens through which even unlived experiences are interpreted.

So, the relationship begins to orbit the symptom. The daughter is remembered not for her curiosity or dreams, but for her fear. And the more the environment sees her through that lens, the harder it becomes for her to separate from that identity.

Supporting, in these cases, does not mean becoming less empathetic. It means **widening the gaze**, letting the person exist in the bond beyond the symptom.

8.5 Make Room for Emotional Expression

For many people with phobias, talking about feelings is not natural. They learned that expressing emotion is risky—being seen as weakness and leading to judgment and rejection. They silence what they feel, not because they feel less, but because they protect more. That silence is a survival strategy. Over time, what finds no words becomes internal weight— and fear ends up carrying what could not be spoken.

Supporting means creating space where emotion can exist without pressure. Not forcing speech, not rushing feelings, but offering a presence that legitimizes experience.

One of the most effective paths is modeling a healthy relationship with emotion: speaking naturally about what you feel, allowing tenderness, joy, and enthusiasm to circulate. It sends an essential message: **feeling is not dangerous.**

And when emotional life has room again, fear stops being the only emotion allowed.

8.6 Breathe to Recover Your Axis

When fear intensifies, one of the first systems to dysregulate is breathing. It speeds up, fragments, becomes shallow and sends a clear message to the body— something is wrong. That is why breathing is not only a relaxation technique, but a direct dialogue with the nervous system.

Conscious breathing helps the organism step out of alarm

and return to a minimal sense of inner control—not because the world changed, but because the body received a different signal: it is possible to slow down.

Throughout this book, you have learned about the R in COURAGE: **Relax and Breathe**. This resource becomes especially important in moments when fear wants to dominate the entire experience. In those instances, regulating together is more important that explaining.

Breathing beside someone—setting a rhythm, offering a calm model—creates co-regulation. The body learns through proximity. When it senses calm breathing in another person, the nervous system finds an external reference that helps it reorganize internally.

And when someone experiences relief through breathing in a moment of fear, that experience does not vanish. The body remembers. Over time, breathing becomes a reliable path back to balance—even when no one is nearby.

Supporting someone who lives with fear is an act of presence—but also of humility. No relationship, however loving, replaces therapy when suffering becomes persistent. Recognizing that limit is a mature form of care.

Emotional pain deserves the same attention as a visible wound—especially when it is expressed in silence. And like any wound, it can heal… or it can become infected if touched without care.

Sometimes what hurts most is not fear itself, but what happens around it: minimizing phrases, jokes that expose, rushed corrections, judging looks. Then the person fights not only the symptom, but the feeling that what they experience is "too much," "ridiculous," or "unbearable" for others.

Language can be fuel—or it can be support.

So, remember: fear feeds on loneliness, urgency, and control; inner support feeds on presence, breath, and meaning. And if today you cannot do it all, return to the essentials: one step, one exhale, one choice. That, too, is courage.

9.
ALIGNING WITH YOURSELF - AND WITH THE WHOLE

This book was born from an encounter with a limit.

Not the limit of fear itself, but the limit that appears when fear stops serving its protective function and begins to occupy a role that does not belong to it: the role of deciding life for you.

Throughout these pages, you have seen that a phobia does not arise in isolation, nor by whim. It takes root when the body learns to react before the person can choose, when an unintegrated experience—personal, relational, or systemic—remains active and repeats itself in the present as if time had never passed. At that point, fear no longer signals danger: it narrows the world, interrupts response, and turns life into a system of avoidance.

That is what appeared—in different ways—in the stories of Jéssica, Maria, Clara, and Talita: fear took on a structural role. Not only as a symptom, but as a way of living—anticipating in order not to feel, restricting in order not to risk, defining what is "possible" in order not to be frustrated, and quietly excluding whatever might have opened life up to what is desired.

And then what hurts most becomes obvious: not fear itself, but the life that stops happening around it. So, if you reached this point hoping for a definitive answer, that makes sense. It is not naïveté—it is exhaustion. It is a need for relief. But clinical work teaches something more honest: fear is not "closed." It is reorganized. And reorganizing it is not an act of force—it is a change of place.

When fear is reorganized, it stops occupying the center from which it shapes identity, decisions, and relationships. In many cases, the phobic object works like a deposit: it holds what is hard to tolerate—vulnerability, uncertainty, exposure, the possibility of failing. In other words, change does not mean "erasing" fear, but expanding your capacity to hold inner experience without automatically translating it into avoidance.

That is what you saw in practice. In all four stories, transformation was not the absence of fear, but the return of response: naming what was being activated, regulating the body, and choosing again. When fear is relocated, it stops deciding life for you—and life begins to move again. Jéssica regained the ability to remain without fleeing. Maria loosened her grip on control. Clara broke a family repetition. Talita made peace with uncertainty.

And that movement—responding again—does not

happen by chance. It requires involvement. Even though there are factors that demonstrably influence the development of a phobia—early experiences, relationships, trauma, neurobiology, context—there is something that cannot be delegated: your part in the process. You did not choose what happened to you, nor your conditions of origin. But staying fixed in guilt tends to lead more to paralysis than to change. Responsibility is not guilt: it is agency reclaimed in the present.

That involvement begins with something concrete: holding what you feel without running. Sometimes fear arrives with a child's voice—a part of you asking for safety in the only way it knows—by activating. The goal is not to silence that part, but to hold it from the inside, regulate the body, and remind it: there is someone here now who can carry this.

And here is a practical truth many people discover late: inner support grows stronger when life has margin. That is why, beyond techniques and exposure, there is a movement that reorganizes the process from within: reclaiming independence. Emotional independence—so that other people do not become your only place of calm—and, as much as possible, practical and financial independence—so your life has air to breathe and room to choose. Because when there is air, fear loses authority: it stops deciding from urgency and becomes a signal you can listen to and move through.

With that margin, something returns that fear often covers: energy to move. Sometimes it shows up as anger, other times, as anguish.

Anger, when understood, becomes direction: it reveals where you make yourself small in order to belong, where you overcarry, where you say "yes" out of fear. Properly oriented, it becomes movement—boundaries, decisions, change.

Anguish often appears when you try to hold everything through control: it is a sign that what is missing is air, body, rhythm. It is not resolved through promises; it is moved through by returning to your center.

If you need a simple compass when fear rises, let it be this: **What am I postponing today that would give me more margin—emotional or practical—and what is the smallest step I can take without handing the steering wheel to fear?**

That is why we insist on the basics: learning to relax, to breathe with intention, and to accept bodily sensations instead of fighting them helps the nervous system come out of survival mode. Acceptance is not resignation. It is regulation. From there, it becomes possible to interrupt automatic thoughts and respond, instead of simply reacting.

That is also why the insistence on reviewing negative thoughts was deliberate. When the mind is dominated by threat, perception narrows and life shrinks. But when inner space opens, desire and vitality reappear—not as something forced, but as the natural effect of greater coherence. Peace, in this sense, is not passivity: it is alignment. When thought, action, and values integrate, inner conflict decreases—and life begins to reorganize.

And motivation changes meaning: it becomes authorship. When threat stops occupying the center, you regain enough room to ask: "What do I want? What matters to me? What do I no longer want to keep postponing?" At first, the answer may be small. But it is real. And when something real returns—an interest, a curiosity, a desire—fear stops being the only engine. Life regains more than one possibility.

Because, deep down, every phobia impoverishes time: it reduces existence to surviving. And life—by its nature—is finite. Remembering that is not becoming dark; it is becoming lucid: understanding that postponing indefinitely does not protect you—it only postpones life. That is why facing fear is not a heroic gesture. It is an act of loyalty to your time, your relationships, and to your life.

And when thoughts appear like "I'd rather avoid," "It's safer not to go," "Better not even try," the essential question is not whether fear is present, but: **Who is deciding right now—me, or my fear?**

Noticing it is not failure; it is waking up. Avoidance never builds resilience: every avoidance quietly confirms fear's authority. Facing does not mean becoming fearless; it means reclaiming authorship over your life. Small choices—conscious and repeated over time—change fear's place: from master to signal.

If at any point you feel you cannot do it alone, asking for help is also courage. Not because you are weak, but because you are choosing not to remain alone inside the same cage.

I will close with something personal, because this book was not born only from theory. I wrote it while looking closely at what a phobia can do when it enters the life of someone we love—how it tries to negotiate the world, reduce it, postpone it.

I wrote it for my husband, who understood that a phobia is not only a limit, but a language. A language that—when deciphered—opens space: new doors, more freedom, a longer path. And I wrote it also for the part of him—and of you—that does not give up. The part that seeks air, movement, and spaciousness, even when fear walks beside it.

I cannot promise you a life without fear. I can offer something more truthful: a life in which fear no longer has the final word. Because life does not require the absence of fear. It asks for presence. And presence, when practiced, becomes home.

REFERENCES

Chapter 1

1. World Health Organization. *Depression and other common mental disorders: Global health estimates* [Internet]. Geneva: World Health Organization; 2017. Available from: https://iris.who.int/server/api/core/bitstreams/6bab42bc-df0f-4f68-a86d-28ebedb85e42/content

2. American Psychiatric Association. DSM-5: *Diagnostic and Statistical Manual of Mental Disorders.* 5th ed. Porto Alegre: Artmed; 2014.

3. Kessler RC, du Pont R, Berglund P, Wittchen H-U. The effects of comorbidity on the onset and persistence of generalized anxiety disorder in the ICPE surveys. *Psychol Med.* 2002; 32(7): 1213–1225. doi: 10.1017/S00332291702006127.

4. Torres AR, Lima MCP. Epidemiology of obsessive-compulsive disorder: A review. *Rev Bras Psiquiatr.* 2005; 27(3): 237–242. doi: 10.1590/S1516-44462005000300015.

5. Breslau N, Kessler RC. The stressor criterion in DSM-IV posttraumatic stress disorder: An empirical investigation. *Biol Psychiatry.* 2001; 50(9): 699–704. doi: 10.1016/S0006-3223(01)01167-2.

6. Ruggiero KJ, McLeer SV, Dixon JF. Sexual abuse characteristics associated with survivor psychopathology. *Child Abuse Negl.* 2000; 24(7): 951–964. doi: 10.1016/S0145-2134(00)00144-7.

7. Kessler RC, Chiu WT, Jin R, Ruscio AM, Shear K, Walters EE. The

epidemiology of panic attacks, panic disorder, and agoraphobia in the National Comorbidity Survey Replication. *Arch Gen Psychiatry.* 2006; 63(4): 415–424. doi: 10.1001/archpsyc.63.4.415.

8. Ibid. The epidemiology of panic attacks, panic disorder, and agoraphobia in the National Comorbidity Survey Replication. Arch. Gen. Psychia – try, 2006, 63(4), p. 415-24.

9. Rosenberg R, Ottosson JO, Bech P, Mellergård M, Rosenberg NK. Validation criteria for panic disorder as a nosological entity. *Acta Psychiatr Scand Suppl.* 1991; 365: 7–17. doi: 10.1111/j.1600-0447.1991. tb03096.x.

9. Ibid.

10. Robins LN, Helzer JE, Weissman MM, Orvaschel H, Gruenberg E, Burke JD Jr, Regier DA. Lifetime prevalence of specific psychiatric disorders in three sites. *Arch Gen Psychiatry.* 1984; 41(10): 949–958. doi: 10.1001/archpsyc.1984.01790210031005

11. Andrade L, Walters EE, Gentil V, Laurenti R. Prevalence of ICD-10 mental disorders in a catchment area in the city of São Paulo, Brazil. *Soc Psychiatry Psychiatr Epidemiol.* 2002;37:316–325.

12. American Psychiatric Association. *Diagnostic and Statistical Manual of Mental Disorders.* 5th ed. Arlington (VA): American Psychiatric Publishing; 2013.

13. American Psychiatric Association. *Diagnostic and Statistical Manual of Mental Disorders.* 5th ed. Arlington, VA: American Psychiatric Publishing; 2013.

14. Fredrikson M, Annas P, Fischer H, Wik G. Gender and age differences in the prevalence of specific fears and phobias. *Behav Res Ther.* 1996; 34(1): 33–39. doi: 10.1016/0005-7967(95)00048-3.

Chapter 3

1. Kessler RC, et al. Lifetime and 12-month prevalence of DSM-III-R psychiatric disorders in the United States: Results from the National Co-

morbidity Survey. *Arch Gen Psychiatry.* 1994; 51: 8–19.

2. Curtis GC, et al. Specific fears and phobias: Epidemiology and classification. *Br J Psychiatry.* 1998; 173: 212–217.

3. Wiederhold BK, Bouchard S. *Advances in Virtual Reality and Anxiety Disorders.* New York: [n.p.]; 2014. p. 91.

4. Ost LG, et al. Exposure in vivo versus applied relaxation in the treatment of blood phobia. *Behav Res Ther.* 1984; 22: 205–216.

5. Agras S, Sylvester D, Oliveau D. The epidemiology of common fears and phobias. *Compr Psychiatry.* 1969; 2: 151–156.

6. Ekeberg O, Seeberg I, Ellertsen BB. A cognitive behavior treatment program for flight phobia, with 6 months and 2 years follow-up. *Nordisk Psykiatrisk Tidsskrift.* 1990; 44: 365–374.

7. Kirkpatrick DR. Age, gender, and patterns of common intense fears among adults. *Behav Res Ther.* 1984; 22: 141–150.

8. Chapman TF. The epidemiology of fears and phobia. In: Davey G, editor. *Phobia: A Handbook of Theory, Research, and Treatment.* London: Wiley; 1997.

9. Rachman S, Taylor S. Analyses of claustrophobia. *J Anxiety Disord.* 1993; 7(14): 51–54.

10. Hetem LAB, Graeff FG. *Anxiety Disorders.* 2nd ed. São Paulo: Atheneu; 2012. p. 127.

11. Ramos RTF. Specific phobias: Classification based on pathophys siology. *Rev Psiquiatr Clín (São Paulo).* 2007; 34(4).

12. Amen D. *Change Your Brain, Change Your Life.* São Paulo: Mercuryo; 2000.

13. Lorenzini R, Sassaroli S. *When Fear Becomes a Disease: How to Recognize and Cure Phobias.* São Paulo: Paulinas; 1999.

14. Rachman SJ. The conditioning theory of fear acquisition: A critical examination. *Behav Ther.* 1977; 15: 375–387; Ost LG, Hugdahl K. Acquisition of phobia and anxiety response patterns in clinical patients. Behav Res Ther. 1981; 19: 439–447.

15. Kay J, Tasman A. *Psychiatry: Behavioral Science and Clinical Foundations*. Nopper E, trans. São Paulo: Manole; 2002. p. 323.

16. Thomas R, Weintraub P. *Babies of Tomorrow: The Art and Science of Parenting*. Caxias do Sul: Millenium; 2004.

17. Lewin BD. Claustrophobia. *Psychoan*. 1935; 4(Quart): 227–233.

18. Bittencourt MIGF. Real space, symbolic space, and childhood fears. *Lat Am J Fundam Psychopathol Online*. 2007; 4(2): 229–237.

19. Gutman L. *What Happens in Our Childhood and What We Do with It*. Córullon M, trans. Rio de Janeiro: Record; 2017.

20. Baptista A. Fear and anxiety disorders: An evolutionary and developmental perspective. In: Soares I, editor. *Developmental Psychopathology: (In)adaptive Trajectories to Throughout Life*. Lisbon: Quarteto; 2002. p. 91–141;

21. Papalia DE, Olds SW, Feldman RD. *The World of the Child*. Lisbon: McGraw Hills; 2001.

Chapter 4

1. Poletti R, Dobbs B. *Resilience: The Art of Bouncing Back*. Rio de Janeiro: Vozes; 2007.

2. Kotler P. *Marketing Management*. 10th ed., 7th reprint. Translated by Maria Silva; technical review by Sapiro A. São Paulo: Prentice Hall; 2000.

3. Giacobbe GC. *Fear is Mental Masturbation*. Rio de Janeiro: Bertrand Brasil; 2011.

4. Freud S. Excerpts from documents addressed to Fliess. In: Freud S. *Brazilian Standard Edition of the Complete Psychological Works of S. Freud*. Salomão J, trans. Rio de Janeiro: Imago; 1980. Vol. 1. pp. 243–380.

5. Freud S. History of an infantile neurosis. In: Freud S. *Brazilian Standard Edition of the Complete Psychological Works of S. Freud*. Salomão J, trans. Rio de Janeiro: Imago; 1980. Vol. 17. p. 19–151.

6. Miller JA. *Lacan's Journey: An Introduction*. Rio de Janeiro: Jorge Zahar; 1987.

7. Solomon S, Greenberg J, Pyszczynski T. *The Worm at the Core: On the Role of Death in Life.* New York: Random House Publishing Group; 2015.

8. Peveler RC, Johnston DW. Subjective and cognitive effects of relaxation. *Behav Res Ther.* 1986; 24(4): 413–419. doi: 10.1016/0005-7967(86)90066-0.

9. Bauer S. *Manual of Ericksonian Hypnotherapy.* Rio de Janeiro: Wak; 2013.

10. Wolpe J. *Practice of Behavioral Therapy.* São Paulo: Brasiliense; 1976. (Original published in 1973.)

Chapter 5

1. Mills V. 180 years of 3D [Internet]. London: The Royal Society; 2018 Aug 13 [cited 2025 Dec 18]. Available from: https://royalsociety.org/blog/2018/08/180-years-of-3d/.

2. Wiederhold BK. Virtual reality in the 1990s: What did we learn? *Cyberpsychol Behav.* 2000; 3(3): 311–314; Lindner P Better, Virtually: The past, present, and future of virtual reality cognitive behavior therapy. *Cogn Behav Ther.* 2021; 50(1): 1–22.

3. Chance P. *Learning and Behavior: Active Learning Edition.* Cengage Learning; 2008.

4. Schwartz MS, Andrasik F, editors. *Biofeedback: A Practitioner's Guide.* 3rd ed. New York: Guilford Press; 2003.

5. Deng X, Wang G, Zhou L, Zhang X, Yang M, Han G, et al. Randomized controlled trial of adjunctive EEG-biofeedback treatment of obsessive-compulsive disorder. *Shanghai Arch Psychiatry.* 2014 Oct; 26(5): 272–279. doi: 10.11919/j.issn.1002-0829.214067.

6. Vargas GC, et al. Freud and Hitchcock: Comparison of phobia cases. *Lat Am J Fundam Psychopathol Online.* 2008; 5(1): 56–68.

7. Agras S, Sylvester D, Oliveau D. The epidemiology of common fears and phobias. *Compr Psychiatry.* 1969; 10: 151–156.

8. Cantón-Dutari A. The use of systematic desensitization in the treat-

ment of fear of flying. *Rev Latinoam Psicol.* 1974; 6: 151–156.

9. Chambless DL, Hunter K, Jackson A. Social anxiety and assertiveness: A comparison of the correlations in phobic and college student samples. *Behav Res Ther.* 1982; 20(4): 403–404. doi: 10.1016/0005-7967(82)90101-2.

Chapter 6

1. Versiani M, Coscarelli P, Andrade Y, Camisão C, Figueira I, Mendlowicz M, et al. Fobia social e depressão. *Jornal Brasileiro de Psiquiatria.* 1994; 43: 673–675.

2. D'El Rey GJF, Freedner JJ. Depression in patients with social phobia. *Psicol Argum.* 2006; 24(46): 71–76.

3. Lydiard RB. Social anxiety disorder: Comorbidity and its implications. *J Clin Psychiatry.* 2001; 62 (Suppl 1): 17–23; discussion 24; Koyuncu A, İnce E, Ertekin E, Tükel R. Comorbidity in social anxiety disorder: Diagnostic and therapeutic challenges. *Drugs Context.* 2019; 8: 212573. doi:10.7573/dic.212573.

4. Ibid.

Chapter 7

1. Gabbard GO. *Psychodynamic Psychiatry in Clinical Practice.* 4th ed. Arlington (VA): American Psychiatric Publishing; 2005.

2. Hellinger B, Ten Hövel G. *Acknowledging What Is: Conversations with Bert Hellinger.* Phoenix (AZ): Zeig, Tucker & Theisen; 1999.

3. Hellinger B, Weber G, Beaumont H. *Love's Hidden Symmetry: What Makes Love Work in Relationships.* Phoenix (AZ): Zeig, Tucker & Theisen; 1998.

4. Erickson MH, Rossi EL, Rossi SI. Hypnotic Realities: *The Induction of Clinical Hypnosis and Forms of Indirect Suggestion.* New York: Irving-

ton Publishers; 1976.

5. Frankl VE. *Man's Search for Meaning: An Introduction to Logotherapy.* 3rd ed. New York: Simon & Schuster; 1984.

Chapter 8

1. Righetti S, Felippe C. Can faith heal? *ComCiência* [Internet]. 2005 [cited 2019 Aug 19]. Available from: http://www.comciencia.br/reportagens/2005/05/06_impr.shtml.

2. Anandarajah G, Mitchell SM. A spirituality and medicine elective for senior medical students: 4 years' experience, evaluation, and expansion to the family medicine residency. *Fam Med.* 2007; 39(5): 313–315.

3 Wolynn M. *It Didn't Start with You: How Inherited Family Trauma Shapes Who We Are and How to End the Cycle.* New York: Viking; 2016.

4 Schützenberger AA. *The Ancestor Syndrome: Transgenerational Psychotherapy and the Hidden Links in the Family Tree.* London: Routledge; 1998.